At the Burning Abyss

THE
SEAGULL
LIBRARY OF
GERMAN
LITERATURE

FRANZ FÜHMANN

At the Burning Abyss

Experiencing the Georg Trakl Poem

TRANSLATED BY ISABEL FARGO COLE

LONDON NEW YORK CALCUTTA

This publication was supported by a grant
from the Goethe-Institut India.

Seagull Books, 2022

Originally published in German as Franz Fühmann,
Vor Feuerschlünden: *Erfahrung mit Georg Trakls Gedicht*
© Hinstorff Verlag, Rostock, 2000, pp. 7–259.

First published in English translation by Seagull Books, 2017
English Translation © Isabel Fargo Cole, 2017

Published as part of the Seagull Library of German Literature, 2022

ISBN 978 1 8030 9 041 2

British Library Cataloguing-in-Publication Data
A catalogue record for this book is available from the
British Library

Typeset in Sabon Linotype by Seagull Books, Calcutta, India
Printed and bound by WordsWorth India, New Delhi, India

CONTENTS

For poems are not feelings, as people think (you have feelings early enough)—they are experiences. For the sake of one poem you must see many cities, people and things, you must understand the animals, feel the birds' flight and know the morning gesture as the little flowers open. You must think back on journeys in strange regions, unexpected encounters and partings you long saw coming—on days in childhood, still unexplained, on the parents you couldn't help hurting when they brought you joy you failed to understand . . . And it is not even enough to have memories. When there are many of them you must forget and have the great patience to wait for their return. For the memories themselves aren't yet it.

Rainer Maria Rilke, *The Notebooks of Malte Laurids Brigge*

My first glimpse of Trakl's appearance—a photographic image, pose of remembrance, barrel-shaped body bent forward, knitted cap sagging over his right ear, smiling obligingly next to his companions—gave me a shock beyond belief. Not, at first, that it was *this* form, but any form at all, any corporeality. Then, too, that it was this one.—Thou shalt make no image; I had none, only his poems, and amid the flux of nearly two decades they had stood as revelations of a fire god: flame shooting down into shadows; blazing thorn bush; föhn and flare; grim glare from hellish depths; now and then the mild glow of sunsets, and beneath the crust of suppression, lava's smouldering incandescence, lowering in fissures.

I needed no image, and when it was forced on me I fended it off, and biographical details too, till I began painfully to see that a poet is also a person and not a mouth alone.

This understanding, which, by the way, I have only lately gained, calls for a sum of experience, and it is of this I wish to tell.

1.

Fire bursting through smoke and darkness, that was my first experience of Trakl: *Under vaults of thorns / O my brother we blind clock-hands climb towards midnight.* —And in this light a poster, plastered back then on every wall: against a smeared grim grey background, a steel-helmeted profile gazing towards a hidden sun, the gesture that signals a tightened chin-strap and below that the solemn appeal to the beholder: The Darkest Hour Is Just Before Dawn!—Now, suddenly, I saw: Towards midnight.

It was 3rd or 4th May 1945, just before the capitulation of the Wehrmacht, and I, a soldier of twenty-three, had through a string of coincidences been released from the military hospital, still hobbling on a stick, to spend a few days scot-free at my parents' with an official pass granting me sick leave and subsequent marching orders to Dresden which lay in ashes somewhere. Probably in enemy territory; the Americans and Russians had met at the Elbe, Berlin was taken, Breslau blasted, Cologne shattered, Hamburg burnt, yet: the darkest hour is just before dawn! And in the mental no-man's-land of a madness that had no more hope, but all the faith in the world, we whispered of the miracle weapons that would annihilate entire armies and waged these battles of annihilation at the pub table amid puddles of beer and streaks of schnapps and demarcation lines of sausage skins, for here in the valleys of the Giant Mountains there was still beer and schnapps and sandwiches, and the still of the night was broken only by drunken singing as the Yankees' and Russkis' conquerors staggered homewards.—Now and then, at vague sounds, we stopped and listened: Were the new bombs' explosions already wresting dawn from the east? But the night kept its silence.—Early next morning I'd have to set out; now, as always after dinner, I sat with my father in his study, each of us immersed in reading, he in fantastical handwritten formulae that he dreamt would bring business to his little pharmacy (such as a poisoned bait for roaming vermin that would stick to their teeth when bitten and couldn't be spat out; or a marvellous rejuvenating elixir in suppository form; or green herbs which, taken as tea, would bring sweet dreams): he, then, in an olive-brown velvet jacket adorned with hussar braid, bent over his magical schemes, and I, already half in uniform, perusing a book of poems purchased in a used bookstore en route from the military hospital, a large-format volume with large type, pale-blue titles over the blocks of verse and on the grey cover a lyre broken by a laurel branch, and through the night behind the window and the eyes this distant lightning flared:

> Over the white pond
> The wild birds have taken flight.

In the evening an icy wind blows from our
stars.

Over our graves
The night bends its broken brow.
Under oak trees we sway on a silver barge.

The city's white walls ring for ever.
Under vaults of thorns
O my brother we blind clock-hands climb
towards midnight.

There was no need for the title, 'Downfall', to tell what this poem voiced.—It was our downfall.— Whenever I read a poem, its images loomed physically before my eyes (I knew no other way to read poetry), and so I saw the pond, and I saw my forest lake, the lake dearest to my heart, at once a piece of the earth's surface with specifiable geographical coordinates and the most secret recess of my soul, but now the forest was a blur of black, and the lake, which in my reminiscent dreams had had the lunar sheen of silver, was now white in the awful sense that it reflected nothing, as chalk reflects nothing, no shore, no tree, not even a sky, mere whitewash, not a ripple stirring now beneath it.—Yet my pond all the same, its singular form.—When I'd discovered this lake—eight years old, on a vacation, having escaped my parents while hiking and lost my way in the unfamiliar forest—its hue was that of the thrill it aroused, the mystery of an enchanted place to be shared with no one. Everyone is granted an experience of this kind; all that matters is not to scorn it. This place can be a cave, an elderflower arbour, a rock crevice, or merely the corner of a room in a certain light, a section of sidewalk over a drain, a basement window, a mountain, a field's edge, a strip of asphalt—for me it was a lake, and its unfathomable depths held the frantic lust of escape as the essence of all possible futures, just as Aladdin's lamp holds the possibility of all power.—And now I learnt that this fullness was gone, transformed into its emptied opposite: the lake filled from the depths with chalk, the rush of the birds in flight still in the air, woods and sky rapidly dimming and an icy wind loosed from our stars.—Our stars were the ones that had shone on our victories, not a certain constellation such as Orion, or the Corona Borealis, but their totality at a certain hour, that of victory, which we believed would return like a dawn that breaks time and again, and now this hour, too, was gone for ever, our stars were nothing but holes in space; cold descended, and although it was May, I knew the white of the pond for the white that appeared in the face of a comrade trudging beside me through the snowstorm, white as a harbinger of life that has frozen to death, a white whose sight makes you wonder if you already bear the same mark.—Death: and cold entered the room; a breath, and I sensed the pond outside the window, and for the blink of an eye I knew, still uncomprehending, that the war was lost.

Readers will sense the narrator's predicament: the infeasibility of relating, in the unfolding of a linear narrative, a moment in which an era that is both outward and inward pools as a second of eternity. And they will have the nagging sense that there is little way to ascertain the account's objectivity: Who can assure them that this is not mere fantasizing, projecting today's insight more than thirty years into the past? These qualms are as impossible to allay as the discomfort with the linear mode of narrative. And so this seems a good occasion for some parenthetical exposition, making the narrative more supportable and addressing the listeners' scruples— we dare not claim to dispel them.

Let us begin with a third thing.

No one who studies Trakl can fail to notice his penchant for colours, and, as some of his interpreters point out, Trakl's colours express and evoke opposing sensations: white is the colour of snow but also that of mould; yellow is gold-like but also faecal; green is May foliage but also the corruption of the flesh, so 'green' implies both hope and fear.—We shall take this opportunity to generalize these observations of Trakl's poetry, grasping the essence of the poetic word as a unity of opposites, even in such unremarkable constructs as 'and' and 'also'.

The German language was so clear-sighted as to give the noun *Wort* [word] two plurals, *Worte* and *Wörter*; from this we shall deduce the existence not of a twofold plural but, rather, of two different though homonymous singulars, henceforth assigning the term *Wort* as the singular form of the plural *Worte* to the realm of the poem, as strictly distinct from a singular *Wort* with the plural *Wörter*, referring to the word as an instrument of scientific study. Here we follow the example of Friedrich Schiller, whose declaration, 'Three words [*Worte*] I call you, weighted with import' refers not to *Worte* in the sense of coined thoughts but to the simple lexemes 'free', 'virtue' and 'God'.[1] But this logic implies nothing less than the existence of two languages, homonymous in their basic elements and yet essentially different, a language of science and of poetry, two languages in which identical-seeming building blocks are utterly different: for example, in scientific usage the adjectives 'red' and 'yellow' must be seen as unambiguous '*Wörter*', that is, as names for the retinal impressions of certain electromagnetic waves, but in the language of the poem as ambivalent *Worte* which, though precisely defined, are inexhaustible. 'Red' is the name for the retinal impression of the frequency 4×10^{14}; and 'red' says a unity of life and death.

'Contradiction', as a word and in a word, provokes readers to contradict: Why should the whiteness of the pond be specified as the white of chalk and frost, when it could just as well be the white of a gentle thing, the white of asters or anemones shivering in the icy wind? Of course the pond can be seen this way too, and Trakl himself provides the best evidence for the various possible readings. This poem is the fifth version of an effort whose four preceding versions have been preserved, showing the following metamorphosis of the pond complex:

Version 1: *Embracing we plunge into blue waters—*

Version 2: *When the coolness of blue waters breathes upon us—*

Version 3: *When the face of stony waters breathes upon us—*

Version 4: *Under the dark vaults of our gloom*
In the evening the shades of dead angels play.
Over the white pond
The wild birds have taken flight—

The third and fourth lines are then adopted as the poem's beginning in its final form. But however we construe the pond's whiteness, don't all the ways of looking at it lead to the same conclusion: an ultimate despair? And isn't this despair so irrefutable because the white in each reading admits *both* interpretations: the pond as a lovely frozen thing, and a lovely thing as something hopelessly threatened by frost?—Trakl's line unites both possibilities (and the word 'white' in itself unites them) by forming the leap between the two, the switching of one to the other within the unity of a poetic image, the exquisitely accurate word for a movement containing a cosmos.

What Trakl has been accused of, what some have been prepared to excuse as 'the urgency of utterance', namely, the use of conflicting adjectival messages in the different versions of his poems—this supposed weakness is his strength, the preternaturally confident use of the poetic word as the elementary building block of all his compositions, the *Wort* in the sense of the plural *Worte* whose essence is the contradictory unity of human experience. Thus each interpretation of poetry is on the right track so long as it is able to embrace at least one element of that unity of contradiction; at the same time, this means relinquishing the claim to be the only right interpretation. Such a one could do no justice to Trakl, let alone those attempts at interpretation that from the outset view a poem not as poetry but as the mere vehicle of a scientific insight, that is, one expressible in *Wörter*.

And should anyone find it suspicious that our interpretation fits a later point in time so perfectly as to suggest that this poem was not written by Georg Trakl in 1913 but, rather, by his interpreter thirty-two or even sixty-four years later, let them see how they respond to this: history, it seems, has followed Trakl's poetry. Without a doubt it has, insofar as Trakl expressed what was to come: the downfall of a world that feels invincible and acts in the belief of this invincibility even as its foundation trembles.—The poem is the other, the anticipatory mode of reality, and the misfortune of the poetic image is that one day it is realized. With that I return to my father's study a few nights before the end of the war.

He sat there in his velvet hussar jacket, sipping wine and scribbling calculations on an empty pack of cigarettes, and over our graves the night bent its broken brow.

—*Over the white pond / The wild birds have taken flight. / In the evening an icy wind blows from our stars. // Over our graves / The night bends its broken brow. / Under oak trees we sway on a silver barge.*—Poems are another kind of dream.—Our graves were the holes that stared in space in our stars' stead: the night, and its broken brow.—I could see it just outside the window and suddenly recalled a scene from a horror movie. The mad owner of a wax museum has lost his face and his mind to a fire that ravaged his business; and so, hiding his charred features beneath a wax mask, seemingly paralysed, appearing only in a wheelchair, he seeks to create a new curiosity cabinet by luring people into his clutches and dousing them with boiling wax. Once, as he tries to overpower a victim, she fights back, his mask shatters beneath her blows and he rears up with the grimace of death emerging from his broken brow.—Women always fainted at this scene; this horror was what kept the cinema going; we sat in our seats, boot-shod juveniles, laughing, cracking jokes, yet feeling the thrill that the madman might grab us—now a veneer cracked again, this time beneath the blows of silence, and I was lifting the book as if to ward them off when suddenly I heard my father ask whether the poems I was reading there, by a Georg Trakl, might be those of a certain Georg Trakl from Salzburg, and when I affirmed that the collection included poems on Mirabell Palace and the Mönchsberg, as well as lines that could refer to an episcopal seat, a gratified smile crossed my father's still-incredulous face;

he stared past his formulae as though the book were an apparition and said with a misty-eyed shake of his head, stroking his hussar braids: So poor Georgie made something of himself after all.

Of course I asked if he knew Trakl, and my father took the book from my hand and leafed through it, explaining that he'd been Trakl's comrade, the same age as he and a military pharmacist too, *Medikamentenakzessist* was the official term, more or less lieutenant rank, strictly speaking a bit higher than a lieutenant, though unfortunately, well, without the same prestige, and he lowered the book and said that as part of a medical battalion deployed in early autumn 1914 near Przemyśl Fortress, he'd often rubbed shoulders with Georgie, eating next to him in the mess hall and sometimes sharing quarters, which was why, if I was interested, he could tell me quite a bit about him; about Georgie's crackpot notions, that loose screw of his, no doubt about it, the chap was crazy, which naturally earned him a proper bit of ragging, and the man of sixty took off his pince-nez and rubbed his eyes, blinded by the sudden light of memory, and blinked and sighed pensively: Dear me, how they used to ride that Georgie, sometimes it was a bit much really, especially how they'd wind him up about his doggerel, his floating corpses and his funny birds, he'd jump up from the table sometimes and couldn't even speak, just swung his fists, and then he'd run out like he was going to do himself harm, but he was that daft, good old Georgie Trakl, you just couldn't help making fun of him, and him a bear of a man, and a good fellow, of course not a good pharmacist, but he could put away the wine like only the staff surgeon could, those were quite some drinking binges back then in Galicia, between one battle and the next, well, and then Georgie suddenly disappeared, probably dismissed, there wasn't much you could do with him really, and all at once, as though fearing thirty years later the guilt of delayed awareness, my father propped the pincenez back upon his nose, cleared his throat, refilled his wine glass and began to read.

The night was outside, its brow riddled with holes, and it and I watched my father lose himself in the poems and quarrel with memories; he'd stare at one line for a long time without moving his eyes, and sometimes he said: 'My God,' and looked up with a helpless smile, and swallowed and read on reluctantly, chewing the ends of his bristly moustache, as he did in awkward moments, and then leafed through the book so distractedly that I both feared and hoped he'd leave off reading with some pleasantry or other, but all at once he nodded vigorously and exclaimed with the eye-widening pleasure of recognition: Yes, that was it, that daft bit of poetry they gave him a hard time about it at a drinking party once, they'd found some of his papers and passed them around in the mess hall and read them out, he remembered now, word for word, and how Georgie bellowed and went red, and white as a sheet, and trembled, so you thought he'd lay about him, bear that he was, but then he just sat there, chalk-white, scary, as if he couldn't hear a thing—and before I could ask which poem he meant, the man in the yellow hussar jacket laughed, genial but raucous, and quoted a phrase and laughed some more and offered his two cents: No sane person could understand that sort of rubbish. But in the midst of his laughter, as though sensing in me the upwelling of that angry sadness that had twice led to blows between us, he broke off and snapped the book shut and proposed a toast to poor Georgie, a good fellow, maybe not a good pharmacist, but undoubtedly the oddest *Medikamentenakzessist* in an Imperial and Royal Austrian Army that never lacked for odd birds.

We drank, and the night watched.—I don't know now, and probably didn't know then, when we raised our glasses and my father silently handed the book back across the table, which poem he'd meant; perhaps one where the sister appears as a monkess, for so I seem to recall the phrase he quoted, but I can't say for certain. All I remember is the toast, and that my father didn't ask what I thought of the poems, whether I liked them, understood them; he turned wordlessly back to his for-mulae, the herb of dreams and the poison in the fox's mouth, burying himself in tomes of organic chemistry, and I felt shy or fearful of asking any more about his comrade, the Imperial and Royal *Medikamentenakzessist*

Georg Trakl, not knowing then that at the time my father believed him dismissed, he had sought refuge in death from the horror of his day, probably by his own hand.— I knew nothing then of the lives of the poets; I wanted no image.—And so I asked no further and took the book and drank wine, and I believe I read once again the poem that had shaken me in the way that leaves cracks you sense will open only later, 'Downfall', its third stanza, the last, never again forgotten: *The city's white walls ring for ever. / Under vaults of thorns / O my brother we blind clock-hands climb towards midnight.*

2.

Under vaults of thorns
O my brother we blind clock-hands climb
towards midnight.

The last two lines of the poem that overwhelmed us—
how to understand them, can we understand them at all,
is 'understand' the right word? Does it describe what
befell us when we first read these lines? Pictures rose
before our eyes, pictures from the poem and pictures
from memory, and pictures from the poem as memory-
pictures, and in memory's picture there are pictures from
the poem, and a force that made us close our eyes, like
truth lifting its head, and a chill down the spine, joining
rapture with horror: is it this meshing of outward and
inward and body and soul that means 'understanding a
poem'? Is receiving a poem, taking it in, the same as
understanding it, or would 'understanding' be the second
stage, a reflective effort following a receptive one, or the
process to begin after this effort, and what would need
to be reflected on? The act of reception, or the thing
received; that is, the poem as something that has already
ceased to be a primal word-form, or this word-form
grasped afresh, cleansed of the defiling emotions and

mood of that passing strange night? But doesn't this process of reflection call for a new receptive embrace, a moment always wonderfully strange in its concrete singularity? We confess: we do not know any of this, nor do we dare plan to unravel it. Trakl's readers have told us about their difficulties with his magical constructs; we merely seek to help them by showing what we went through with these lines, which means showing what we went through when we, too, felt the need for what is generally called understanding. This need amounted to a wish to resolve poetry into rationality, to grasp the ambiguous unambiguously, that is, to convert a construct of *Worte* into a construct of *Wörter*.—We tried desperately, to the point of destroying the poem; *this* was an experience too. It fell short of what 'understanding' can be, but perhaps it was essential.

First, though, we had better amend one statement. We said that, for us, taking in a poem meant physically seeing the images bespoken by its words. This needs to be put more concretely: How can you picture 'the wild birds *have taken* flight'? If you see them taking flight, you don't see the pond deserted; if you see it deserted, you don't see the birds.—A poem isn't a sketch for a painting, it's something like the kernel of a film: consummate and self-contained, yet open, carte blanche for dreaming. But we don't dream in images alone, we dream in emotions and bodily sensations, and we dream in concepts, if there is something that is to an ordinary concept as *Worte* are to *Wörter* (we confess that we lack the corresponding term). We can settle on 'meaning' and perhaps on 'sense', if we seek to see this as a word's concrete ambiguity, its freightedness with all experience, rather than aiming at a single meaning as the sole correct interpretation. Mind you: the *concrete* ambiguity, which, for all its fullness, is as uniquely precise as the word that carries its freight in the smallest possible space and, fitted into the whole of the poem, contributes to this whole just as the whole shapes it in turn.—For example, 'vaults of thorns' is not 'blossom' or 'star' or 'lion' or 'water', it is 'vaults of thorns', yet it is fraught with every experience that humanity and all individuals have ever had with vaults of thorns or ever will in future: arching brambles; the drops of blood in the green of every childhood; 'The Jew among Thorns' from the Grimms' cruel tales; the pointed arch of a cathedral; winter over a mansion gate; Titian's rusty brown in *The Crowning with Thorns*; the barbed wire of an obstacle course; the sleep of Briar Rose; a section of border fence; the carved crossed beams adorning the roof of a fisherman's hut; the shrike's hedge; the voice calling Moses from the burning bush; the first awful humiliation; a witch's bed; a folksong; a sudden vision of Bluebeard's chamber—all these and many more such things that we can't even imagine might appear as the picture of this word, and each concrete embodiment simultaneously holds the latency of all its possibilities, so what is the sense in arguing about the right interpretation? This dispute has been waged about 'vaults of thorns' too:

tracery or tendril, architecture or botany, how are we to see the image of these words, or—speaking with the madness of the interpreter—how was it meant by the poet himself? To us such disputes seem futile. The dream sees—or, better, knows—or, better yet, has in store all forms in one: that *is* the dream-form, distinct from the real one. The dreamer beholds one through the other, the filaments in the tracery, the stone in the tendril, a thought construct in both; a poem operates in analogous fashion. Always transcending the intent of its creator, which anyway is ultimately inaccessible to others, it can invoke —just as a dream mingles image, emotion and concept— all the reader's physical and ideational experiences with vaults of thorns, as well as the symbolism of the unconscious and of personal mythology.

A poem meshes the fantastically precise and the inexhaustible to create a unique new form. And if we can settle on the concept of understanding as a simultaneous broadening and focusing of our consciousness that enables us to intuit the infinitude of a poem while grasping its specificity (which, and which alone, gives it personhood in the realm of word-forms) at one of the points, at least, where the part most vividly exemplifies the nature of the whole (though really this would be everywhere)—then we'd gladly give everything to understand a poem.—Let the poem's crystalline precision keep us from straying in a bad infinitude, and in the intuition of its infinitude we shall not fear analytical precision, indeed we must insist on it to do justice to the poem, to its word-form, each of its stanzas and each of its lines and each of its words: 'Under', 'vaults', 'of', 'thorns', 'O', 'my', 'brother', 'we', 'blind', 'clock-hands', 'climb', 'towards', 'midnight'.

Let us take the very least thing: *Under vaults of thorns*—what does 'under' mean, how are we to see the image of these words?—The question seems foolish, the image quite clear: vaults of thorns, and under them the clock-hands. But the 'under' proves equivocal: the clock-hands might lie under the thorns like an eye under the brow, that is, in a two-dimensional image the upper- and the undermost would be so completely separated that each appears in the full form of its frontal view, the upper crowning the lower. Yet, too, the clock-hands might lie under the thorns as the eye lies under the closed lid, so that in the two-dimensional image Over would overlie the Under. A combination of these two situations is also conceivable—but these are mere externalities, topographic; a line of poetry is more than that.—'Under' as a *Wort* with the plural *Wörter* would entail, in this connection, a merely geometric relationship; however, 'under' as a *Wort* with the plural *Worte* invokes a cosmic order as well, setting up hierarchical values within it: an Above, a Below and a division into ranks. This takes place twice in each of the poem's nine lines: *Over the white pond—Over our graves—Under oak trees—Under vaults of thorns*. Then come the slanted lines of motion: *from our stars*, from above to below; *towards midnight*, the countermovement; from above to below the icy wind;

from below to above the blind clock-hands climbing, and the meeting place: *midnight*.—If 'under' had merely topological force, one could accuse the poet of imprecision for letting his line contain a contradiction.—Under vaults of thorns: Torment? Shelter? Ornament? Or all of these, or everything? Not 'everything'; merely 'Under vaults of thorns'. But doesn't the space between shelter and torment encompass our whole world?

Strange—we recall it clearly—strange that when the image of these lines appeared to us back then, we did not see the vaults of thorns; they must have been so immediate a presence that we had no need to behold them incarnate: We *were* under them, so how could we see them?—What we saw were gargantuan walls of wet, black blocks, seamlessly stacked and smoothly trimmed, the clock's circle a mere knowledge of numbers in its empty, unmarked compass; and where the 'twelve' of midnight should have stood was a gaping black hole towards which we desperately struggled, blind clock-hands; this 'blind' appalled me.—Clock-hands show an hour they cannot see themselves: Which hour did we reveal? These lines lashed me with scorpions: 'brother' meant me; my 'I' climbed along with the 'we'; but we weren't climbing towards our downfall, were we, we were trying to stave it off with all the agonized exertion contained in the word 'climb'—why did this line dismay me so?—'They hold only their face into time, and as though under water, they cannot see',[2] once these lines of Rilke's had perturbed me; now I read the same thing, darker, and the earth trembled. Into what confusion was I plunged? Bent over this poem, I'd understood for the eternity of a moment that we had lost the war, yet like each previous premonition this still-subconscious understanding had turned to the delusion of a victory against the odds, an automatism of desperate self-deception suddenly held up before me in the line: *blind clock-hands climb towards midnight.* It was as though Trakl's poem began as an *I* to rise up against me and—paralysed and affected, yet already savouring this paralysis as liberation —I watched the struggle with dreamlike equanimity: *Under oak trees we sway on a silver barge.*—Under the oak trees hanged men swayed, even in our quiet valley.

That was early May 1945; it was not much longer before I grasped this very delusion of ours as the essence of blindness and realized, shuddering, that we blind clock-hands had indeed climbed with desperate strength towards midnight. But what disturbed me still more, much later: The poet himself *saw* the clock-hand, and *saw* midnight, and *saw* himself, and yet, self-seeing, could see himself as blind?—Was it the blindness of an eye within the eye, or the blindness of the old seers, the blindness of Tiresias?—It took a long time to realize that what Trakl invoked was a blindness incapable of looking past its own time; the blindness of all the gifted ones who have eyes to behold themselves and whose boldest gaze sees: blind clock-hands.—Here we shall stop.

The street was silent when I left the house; wan darkness, no stars; from the doorway where my parents waved the hall light, mocking blackout regulations, welled cloudy in the mild air.—To this day I hear my father saying as we hugged goodbye and afterwards, as I went down the front steps typical of mountain homes, that next time he'd tell me much, much more about Georgie, it was all coming back to him, such odd and droll things; he'd fill me in after the war was won.—I never saw my father again: he died a few days later, reportedly of blood poisoning, though I suspect he resorted to one of his vials; at any rate that was our last conversation. He left behind no writings and doubtless wouldn't have thought it worth the effort to note down memories of his crazy bunkmate. Though he'd told me more about Georgie that night, I can vouch only for what I related above and for one other detail which I believe my father shared, though I later found it recorded in another source, in Albert Ehrenstein's remembrances: leaning of out the window at dusk, Trakl loved to toss a glowing cigarette stub on the street and watch it fade.—The same movement is found in some of his poems, the quiet passing of a small tranquillity amid all the indifferent forces that are like night vanquishing the evening—*Fled is the gold of the days, / The evening's brown and blue shades: / The shepherd's flutes have died away / And evening's blue and brown shades / Fled is the gold of the days*—and a consciousness that preserves this fading.

I turned off into total darkness; water rushed far below the street.—Was I thinking of Trakl? I hurried to the station, where the trains were still running; it was a long way, an hour at least, and I was still hobbling on a stick. I was probably humming one of the idiotic verses that you use to drum yourself into the trance of automatized marching, a mercenary's verse, a mercenary's tune; all I recall is my hounded haste in the warm, dark night. But I know that premonition and madness and lurking fear were already solidifying into the figure of an angel, often invoked in those days, regularly by my father: Michael, the angel of the Germans, would cleave the heavens with his sword and descend to save his people, clad in flaming armour, at the final hour when night is darkest.—I had never seen Michael as a guardian angel; even before that May he was the Angel of the Apocalypse, the angel of the sixth trumpet and the falling fire who proclaims in all the tongues of the Earth: Babylon the great is fallen, is fallen, and is become the habitation of devils, and the hold of every foul spirit, and a cage of every unclean and hateful bird, Babylon the great is fallen, is fallen; all nations have drunk of the wine of the wrath of her fornication!—I'd grown terribly familiar with this angel now that fire had fallen from the sky, an envoy with pinions of snow and temples of scarlet; the angel of my heart was gentle and pure but now his wings were stained with faeces and worms dripped from his lids; in this shape, I took Trakl with me.—And I still carried in my knapsack the large grey book with the broken lyre on the cover, for five or six days more, then tossed it away along with my knapsack, coat, blanket and tinned meat in the hope of making it more quickly to the Americans who were said to have halted at the Elbe.

All the people hastening through Bohemian forests strove to reach the Americans; the war was over; no angels appeared; beneath the oaks and the spruce, the SS marauded and the henchmen of a southward-fleeing field marshal court-martialled and hanged the northward-fleeing soldiers; and tens of thousands of POWs trotted eastward, steps dragging, heads hanging, to meet an inconceivable fate. Since that fate was not the instant execution we had anticipated, it could only mean that young and old would spend the rest of their lives in the Siberian lead mines.—It was the end of Nazism, and we did not doubt the downfall of the thing we called Germany; it was what we were experiencing.—The war was lost; no angels appeared; the way to the Elbe was blocked by a victor whose wells we had choked with dirt, whose apple trees we had felled, whose mines we had flooded, whose cities we had burnt down—he would take his revenge now, no doubt about it.—At this hour each saw a dark omen—mine was an icy cattle car filled with singing Ukrainian women, rolling off into the grey of a February dawn—and we tore the insignia from our uniform shirts, the officers shed their epaulettes, the military police their glittering gorgets, and here and there the SS with glowing iron expunged their sigils from their own flesh.—What was left was a void; it expanded.—

Hastening westward through the woods to the Elbe, I hoped to join some foreign legion; I was twenty-three and had my A levels, taken early due to the war, but all I could do was operate a machine gun, obey and carry out orders; some colonial service might be able to use me, that was my final hope, now that Germany was a hope no longer. But on all the roads to the Elbe and surrounding the woods soldiers stood in long, earth-brown coats with long bayonets on their guns; their watch fires smoked, they drank and laughed, bells pealed, now and then a machine gun stuttered, and hanged men swayed from the oaks.—A suicide attempt in the brush by a field and my last escape had failed, and I trotted with the ten thousand eastward for seventeen days, sun stabbing, cherry trees blooming; we ate their sap and ate the grass where we bivouacked and swam in the streams and ponds and ate water and ate dirt and heard the bells from the Moravian steeples and stared into the alien, yet already unbelievably familiar, faces of the young Kirghiz soldiers who escorted us, and it was May.—In those days I thought nothing; it was a sense of perfect lightness, of floating in an empty space.—No longer here, not yet there.—After swimming we lay naked in the sun, animal torpor beyond hunger and despair, perhaps, for a few days, the bliss of nothingness.—I owned only what I carried on my person, and that was little: belt and boots still, coat no longer, no watch, no lighter, no pen, no knife and no book; that lay somewhere by the side of the road, a knapsack filled with tinned meat and Trakl's poems. I didn't even wonder whether someone would find and read it, I thought nothing.

And yet I carried these poems with me as a wan glow against which I now saw the world. Just as you see a landscape at sunset, in murky November, when fog and red glow mingle in a smouldering dusk where trees and houses loom blocked in black, nearby nothing but black, faraway things indistinguishable: a fading into the realm of shadows, yet an unreal light prevailing in the consciousness of nearing night.—*Twilight and decay*; it was May, the cherry trees were blooming and we trotted, grey with hunger and dread, towards the east, to a reception camp near Brno where we were interrogated and shorn and received; in place of the confiscated pay-book, the abbreviation for *voyennoplenny* in yellow oil paint on the back of our uniform jackets and on our trouser legs and on our caps; this was our new home, and there was food for the first time and I crouched in the mud outside the overfilled barracks and dunked dry bread in the millet soup and heard the silent din of the lines:

> *There is a light, extinguished by the wind.*
> *There is a field of stubble, where a black rain*
> *   falls.*
> *There is a vineyard, burnt and black with*
> *   holes full of spiders.*
> *There is the road towards downfall.*

These were Trakl's verses, mingled with lines of my own, relentless droning litany of a fading consciousness seeking self-pity as its sole crutch.—So I took Trakl into captivity and my brooding and despair wore his colours: shadows embracing in front of a mirror gone blind, former lives slipping past on silver soles.—This was Trakl's 'Psalm', which I learnt by heart back then; for a long time I kept it in my memory, and had I been asked in summer 1945, in the convoy from the Brno transit camp to the labour camp at Neftegorsk in the Caucasus, what the seminal event of my last few years had been, I would have replied without hesitation: The discovery of Georg Trakl's poem.

It seems high time to return to the reader's question: what real certainty can he have of not being manipulated by our interpretation? Isn't it absurd, he'll ask, genuinely indignant now, to present Trakl's 'Downfall', written in 1913, as though he had intended the midnight towards which the blind clock-hands climb to mean the day of the Wehrmacht's surrender?—Of course that would be absurd, but we do not claim to know what Trakl really might have meant, we are merely recounting our experience, albeit as precisely as possible.

Trakl's poem is not a poem à clef, not an account of something that occurred before the time of writing, such as the sinking of the Titanic, nor is it an augury in the sense of anticipating such an account, though it does prophesy something.—It prophesies what is already there, unseen; in his poem it enters the consciousness, but this 'it' is not a fact to be pinned down in place or time.—

His poem is not an allegory; it models a downfall that is a process, not a result. 'Climb' is in the present tense, not the past or the future, and everyone who feels affected is free to find himself in this image, that is, to see what is happening to him.—This process unfolds both outwardly and inwardly; as long as these two things remain aligned, the poem affects us in its concreteness, yet the concreteness lies not in a representational congruence with some purely objective thing but in the precision of the poetic images, whose logic, both separately and taken together, represents that very process; and so the meaning takes form.—A helpful mental construct.—The grand old man of modern mythology, Karl Kerényi, once remarked that it is in the nature of myths, though not created as explanations, to be explanatory. Poems are similar: it is in their nature to signify concrete things without having been written for that purpose, for they negate themselves when they signify, just as myths negate themselves when they explain.

Towards which midnight do the blind clock-hands climb?—Not towards some exact time of day, much less on some determinable date. 'Midnight'—as the name for that point in time, recurring in a twenty-four-hour rhythm, when the sun (with respect to a given location) reaches its lowest point below the horizon, hence also as the name for the last segment of a day, a concrete Day X—is a *Wort* with the plural *Wörter*; and even as a name for that point in time when 24:00 on Day X is simultaneously 00:00 on Day X + 1, 'midnight' remains such a word, though its character is already destabilized by the now-ambivalent definition. As a *Wort* with the plural *Worte*, 'midnight' continues to designate a spatially manifested final hour as well as the coincidence of two different courses of time (unforgettably put in Eduard Mörike's 'Midnight': 'they sing in the ear of their mother, the night / of the day / *that today has been*'). But while this exhausts the meaning of 'midnight' as a *Wort* with the plural *Wörter*, the homonymous *Wort* with the plural *Worte* is only the starting point from which the meaning now unfolds in all its fullness as both a temporal and a spatial concept.—The character of the instant is transformed from a moment on the calendar to a moment in eternity that can last for generations, and if 'midnight' as a *Wort* with the plural *Wörter* designates nothing but the point at which the end and beginning of two days coincide, only to part at once as past and present, the midnight of the *Wort* with the plural *Worte* is the emergence—still retaining chronometric alignment—of one particular hour from the uniform flow, the wave crest of a time running counter to what tradition holds as the only valid time. Now, reversing all that time's prevailing values, a counter-world yawns: the sulphurous counter-noon as Satan appears in the witches' circle to establish, at least till the stroke of one, or perhaps till cockcrow, his realm, which is in the world and yet not: in and in addition to that one world, the Other.—What will happen at the moment when the clock-hands align and a wheelwork is set in motion to strike the hour that will be midnight, a long way still from one o'clock?—Blind clock-hands, they don't see, though they point.

From this cloud of possibilities the flash of revelation struck us: midnight, for us, was the black gate towards which we climbed in order to plunge into the void, into the supreme darkness that blots out all hope and faith; at the same time this poem plunged us into the obscurity of an enigmatic rapture whose nature did not dawn on us until much, much later. This rapture has remained, provoking us to ask whether midnight mustn't simultaneously be conceived as the noon of the night; that is, Arcanum and uncanny, the time when 'all songs of loving ones awake' and 'all gushing fountains speak louder':[3] 'O man! Take heed! / What saith deep midnight's voice indeed? / I slept my sleep— / From deepest dream I've woke and plead:— / The world is deep, / And deeper than the day could read. / Deep is its woe— / Joy—deeper still than grief can be: / Woe saith: Hence! Go! / But joys all want eternity— / Want deep profound eternity!'[4]—just as the joys of witches want it.

Towards which midnight do the blind clock-hands climb?—Towards that voiced by the *whole* poem, 'Downfall', in which we sway in a silver barge under oak trees.—One does these nine lines little justice by reading them as a ballad, as a sequence of events whose first is the flight of the wild birds and whose last, after swaying on a silver barge, would be the climb towards midnight, towards downfall.—This downfall is the simultaneity of all that seems irreconcilable: that we sway on a silver barge under oak trees while the night bends its broken brow over our graves, and that the city's white walls ring for ever while an icy wind blows from our stars. The wild birds have taken flight, and from here on all the verbs are in the present tense: all the events in its nine lines are present together, and present with the time of all the readers they affect.—The present is simultaneity, yet the simultaneity of a poem is more than just inert juxtaposition; poetic logic links the meanings and 'we' reconciles the irreconcilable: our swaying under oak trees on a silver barge is our climbing towards midnight under vaults of thorns, towards a future that we ourselves prepare, with shudders, yet by our own will. 'Climb' speaks of strenuous effort, and 'sway on a silver barge' speaks of joy.

Trakl's nine lines were written at a time when public consciousness was lulled by the delusion of unshakeable security and one of its representatives never ceased to proclaim: 'I shall lead you to glorious times!'—The words of Kaiser Wilhelm II; some of his contemporaries read the era differently. 'My religion is the belief that the manometer has hit 99', wrote Karl Kraus in 'Apocalypse' in 1908. And Hans Davidsohn alias Jakob van Hoddis wrote in 1911: 'The philistine's hat whirls off before his eyes, / The airs resound as though with screams, / Workers fall from roofs and smash to smithereens, / And on the coast, we read, the tide is on the rise.' Two years later, another of his and Trakl's generation, Alfred

Lichtenstein, wrote: 'Some day—the writing's on the wall— / Death shall sweep down with northern winds. / The smell of corpses casts a pall. / And murder's tyranny begins.'—The north is midnight's realm, but Trakl's poem is called 'Downfall', not 'World's End' like the poem by Jakob van Hoddis; it does not speak of destruction by flood, steel or fire but of what happens to you and me as we drift towards an end that might take such a form.— Midnight is End Time and one day will be the Last Time, but what will then be a storm is, for now, a wind from our stars; the wild birds have taken flight but the city's white walls still ring and the fountains speak louder; and in the minute before midnight, blind Faust in the delusion of noon hears the clinking of shovels and dreams the great dream of a free people on free soil while Mephisto and the grave-digging lemurs whisper to each other: 'The clock has stopped— / Has stopped! Like midnight, all life is diminished. / The hand has fallen. / Fallen, it is finished. / It is all over. / Over! What a stupid name. / Why over? / Over and pure nothing, it is all the same.'[5]

But that is a dream of Mephisto's.

Above the rust mud of the Novorossiysk harbour, as we staggered from the freighter's belly, staring aghast at the rubble of the city on the green-red flank of the Caucasus, and the sudden rumour arose that this was *our* city, that we would remain captive here until it was rebuilt, thirty, fifty, a hundred years—above us, on one of the ramp's rails, bombed to a spiral, some member of the victor's

peoples, an older fellow, half-naked, part of a troop dis-
entangling a snarl of iron with their bare hands, cried to
us with a laugh from the heart that we'd now sleep man
with men, and he cried that many in Russia slept that
way, in the camps behind barbed wire, men with men,
without women, all their lives, and he laughed and
swayed his sweat-slick torso and, repeating his words,
slammed his hollowed right fist on his upstretched left
thumb; there was a smacking sound; his comrades
laughed and the ruins of the marble-white city lay
beneath the crystal of the sky.—Its walls no longer rang;
did I think of Trakl? Everything was possible in this hour
and things never believed possible had occurred.—The
most unbelievable thing was that we were alive; it
mocked all prophecies.—Nothing came as expected:
What had become of us?

I have tried again and again to put to paper that
singular era of the POW, the VOYENNOPLENNY, and
each time the very beginning confounded me, that
moment of utter openness when past and future, no
longer mere modes of physical time, begin to reveal
themselves as historical forces, when their ever-fluid
boundary gapes as a chasm so profound that the *I* ruptures too, and to negotiate this rupture a process begins:
transformation. With fantastic rapidity, the present
becomes openness in all directions, even into the past.
It is the moment of a leap, describable only through the
most precise possible Before and After, and between them
the sum of possibilities without which no After can be

grasped.—This transformation takes many forms; the leap (which can also lead into the past) lasts minutes to decades. Some may be spared it entirely; I do not envy them.

The first thing to plunge into my chasm was abstract, categorical thinking (to the extent that I had any command thereof); what burst forth from it was a wild curiosity, lust for the new, unheard-of things—for the old had ended and life went on nonetheless—that would inevitably begin on this coast.—The stink of burning, hunger, barbed wire, no matter.—Men sleeping with men; this avowal too was new and utterly unheard-of: male homosexuality, soldiers' everyday secret temptation, was viewed in the past as the epitome of disgrace and transgression. Then was this vast land truly, in a different way, the realm of all re-evaluated values? Stalin's smile on a poster taller than a man; what Otherness were we entering?—I knew nothing and was aflame for everything, for faces, for words, for events, for books; and for this landscape too, different from anything I had known: an intuition of glaciers, stagnant sea.

Possibly I thought of Trakl, I certainly saw his angel; I am sure I can recall the torso of an angel lying in the ruins we'd been shuffling through for hours, amid the rubble of columns and balconies—but who knows memory's will.—We know nothing of the mental metabolism; the physical process, it's said, can be traced with atomic markers, telling us which cells a certain substance nourishes, but who knows how poetry works when its metaphors surge through the veins of the unconscious? What action or thought do they feed, what do they make ready, what do they store, in which strong rooms and under which ciphers?—We know nothing and assert so much.—Probably no angel lay in the rubble, and only my memory puts him there now, but that need not make my memory false: the angel was inside, then, not outside, and poetry is bound up with both.—The angel in the rubble had shattered wings; his boyish face was twisted with pain; there were faeces on his shoulder.—Smiling lips; he seemed to be holding his tongue.—The footpath climbed past the ruins; scree, shot through by prickling grasses; I know that hunger bellowed like a bull and that in the evening we stewed snails, a foaming, faecal, stinking meal, and the sky lay yellow on the shimmering sea.—A puddle of oil; one spark and it would burn; I wished it would, the night was cold.—Our fires faded; did I think of Trakl? Certainly I did not, in the sense that his name came to mind; certainly I did, in the sense that in every feeling, even in my rat-like hunger that kept me awake like the others, something of his verses stirred. Poetry works upon a person as a whole, and if it is unforgettable, that can only mean it works steadily and inescapably, whether you sense its presence or not.— Then you unconsciously see World in the poetic images that brought World to your consciousness; indeed, you live poems without knowing it, aware of nothing but your life: unformed moments whose coalescence into figures (and myths) long remains obscure, often utterly so.—If someone has been overwhelmed by poetry, it works throughout his future, and if there is night in that poetry, each night he lives will also be its night, not *only* its night but *also* its night.—Lived interpretation.— *Herdsmen buried the sun in the bare woods*—here we buried it as a hundred fires in pits of stone, we buried suns, and though I had some sense of this burial, I would puzzle over the line for a long time yet to come.

Later, after the news of Auschwitz, when we fled the truth about our past in self-lamentation and felt our present to be senseless, an undeserved doom that had descended to grind us down with hunger, mud-shovelling, freezing, idling, homesickness, tedium, uncertainty, and hunger yet again, and hunger all the time, to the point of such physical exhaustion that no one but the fat cook could even have desired to sleep man-with-men, and the future lay as a white pond, a chalk-filled pit— later, as something to cling on to, I thought up exercises about colours: 'blue', for example. I tried to tell myself all the things that were blue: litmus paper dipped in an alkaline solution, amethyst, lapis lazuli, turquoise, the British colonies in the old atlas, the Grotta Azzurra, bellflowers, gentians, the outside of the Virgin's robe in icons, air-force collar patches, cornflowers, larkspur, noble blood, the blood in the veins, baboon buttocks, baby clothes for boys, the Rhine, the Danube, bruises after fistfights, the tongues of Chow Chows, alcohol flames, the mountains, the Adriatic, stewed red cabbage, blueberries, bluethroats, Freya's eyes, Apollo's hair, veronica, Prussian blue, sea blue, navy blue, laundry blue, royal blue, kingfisher blue, the will-o'-the-wisp's wings; and abstractions too: faith, loyalty, the south, the distance, forgetfulness, longing, the twilight of the soul. Inventory of the schoolboy—were they Trakl's colours?—They were not and yet they were: his poem had merged with my life, how could I sift out one from the other now? No sieve can do such a thing.

But just as his verse entered my existence, my thoughts entered his verse and made it wretched: I invoked it in my wretchedness. I'd traded two portions of bread for the stub of an ink pencil and I owned one of the sanded-smooth shingles which, due to the total lack of paper, served for the camp's card file and the correspondence between the *Kommandantura* and the self-administration of the *plenny*, so I hunkered every evening on my cot, on the bracken-filled mattress, and scribbled poems which I had to scratch away the next evening (I owned a shard of glass as well) in order to write new ones, and I wrote of decay and downfall, of the end of Europe and the fall of the angel, of a vineyard with holes full of spiders and God's icy breath and the lost paradise; I wrote into the void in miniscule letters, and I wrote 'Brother Trakl'.—Was he my brother?—He had entered my *I*, how could he not be my brother? It wasn't Trakl alone whose verses returned to my mind; there, too, lived Josef Weinheber, Rilke, Stefan George, my gods before him, and still sacred, but I would have called none of them 'brother'.—Was I wrong to invoke Trakl? I admit that even now I'm at a loss; a helplessness of feeling; logic, at any rate, is against me.—But isn't the work always that which works, and can you pick and choose how something works on you?

I see myself hunkered on the cot, I see a long wooden barrack, a floor of rammed earth, a heating stove in the middle, tiny windows, bunk beds: mine is the bottom bunk by the door which opens away from me and opens often, the draftiest sleeping-place; I huddle with the tin of soup between belly and thighs; the slimy black bread has already been devoured; the night outside the door is a dozen shuffling feet and I scratch last night's poems from my shingle, skimming the rhymes one last time: ' . . . from afar / . . . lamenting call / . . . icy star / . . . our downfall', and now from afar I see a column of black smoke and it smells of burnt human flesh. For a long time I'd refused to see it; I was fleeing from myself, while it was all the way inside, and I was seeking all the blame outside me.—I was hungry and cold; so how could I be to blame?—I cut a sorrowful and sorry figure.—Some day I shall write down the *whole* of this time with all its prodigious grotesqueness and grandeur, tragedy and bur- lesque, liberation and entrapment; here I can speak only of Trakl, but when I call him my brother, this smoke belongs to him as well. That stele of barbarism, more lasting than all bronze monuments—he saw it looming, not over Europe, only over the fen's reeds, and this fen *was* Europe: *A deer bleeds softly by the wood / And ravens splash in bloody gutters. / Rank growth of yellow reed-grass flutters. / Frost, smoke, a step in empty woods.*—No, it's a mere winter scene, but it is also the winter of the soul.—A step in empty woods; who is approaching?—The Stone Guest who comes uninvited, and no adjuration can turn him away.—I refused to believe in Auschwitz, refused to hear of any blame; I buried myself in self-pity and laments and recited Trakl's verses, but how can you tell yourself without consequences: *There is a vineyard, burnt and black with holes full of spiders. / There is a room, and they've whitewashed it with milk?*—I was not conscious of asking who had burnt the vineyard, whitewashed the room, defiled the milk, but that does not mean that these questions were not asked.—What were the spiders that dwelt in my heart?—I wanted to remember Trakl's poems, not my past, but who knows memory's will? What does it choose, what does it suppress, what does it examine, what does it make ready?

For sure, the verses I recalled fed my laments, but they goaded on another thing that began to fight against me and for me.—Nothing entered my consciousness, but what does that prove?—One day in the winter, when a former Buchenwald inmate told how the camp commander had kept a private zoo with beasts of prey, I felt the earth quake and an image forgotten for two years loomed, an episode on the retreat from Greece: I saw myself behind the bars of the cage and this image refused to go away; later it became a story. What was that image during those two years: a blank, because it did not appear in my consciousness? It did nothing but wait within me, but waiting is also working, just as lava waits inside a volcano, preparing to erupt. And Trakl's poetry was not resting in oblivion; I moved it through my memory and forced it to rise and fall—would it have done so except according to my will?—When I measure this will against that poetry, I cannot believe that, not only because of the disparity between the two. How can a poem bring its contradiction to fruition if not by causing a conflict within the reader? And if the reader's will takes one side, the unconscious takes the other. To capture the unity of the contradiction, you are reduced to drawing conclusions *ex contrario* from the recollected figures of consciousness; without them the process as a whole cannot be grasped, and sudden developments remain inexplicable.—Continuous ones as well.

All the angels I pinned down on my shingles were radiant forms, even in falling, glowing, glimmering, in fluttering flame; where had their soiled brother been banned to?—Six years later he stepped forth once again; of his existence during that time I know only this: he cannot have been idle.

We cannot concur strongly enough that it would limit one's understanding of Trakl's work to regard him solely, or even chiefly, as a Christian poet; this term does him as little justice as it does for Hölderlin.—Undoubtedly the angel or the *bread and wine* that shine out again and again, bright and pure, in their work are eminently Christian symbols, but first of all they are bread and wine as the fare of everyday rural life which in Catholic countries includes angels, though mainly in a trivialized form: over children's beds, on bridges and squares, in wood carvings, in figures of speech, not to mention in the always-open churches. Above and beyond the everyday, they are far-reaching symbols. Christian things have their uniqueness, one must guard against hasty conclusions that can shut important doors.

Trakl was a Protestant and when he felt provoked he professed his faith pugnaciously; he often referred to himself as a Christian. According to a famous anecdote, at a rural parish fair he pointed aghast at the first prize at the raffle, a bloody calf's head, saying: 'Our Lord Jesus!' But what these biographical traits prove is that Christian mythologems come readily to an expanded consciousness; they appear in Trakl's work too, and while it would be petty to deny them, to exalt this plane of reference as transporting the one true meaning, like one school of interpreters, would be narrow-minded. And what might that be, a profession of Christianity? The source of the anecdote, Karl Röck of Innsbruck, added in his 'Diary, Summer 1913': 'Due to these appalling words, which were naturally incomprehensible to their stolid emotional sobriety and thus appeared to them as sheer blasphemy, they (the farmers) wanted to expel him.'⁶—The Swiss writer Hans Limbach recounted something equally provocative in his diary, a remark Trakl made in conversation one evening, 'It's unheard-of . . . how Christ, with each simple statement, solves the deepest questions of humanity! Can the question of the communion between man and woman be solved more fully than by the commandment: *The twain shall be one flesh*?' In Trakl's poetry they *are* one flesh; does that make him a Christian poet? The question sounds as blasphemous as the exclamation at that parish fair, yet it is meant in earnest.

We should recall that our culture is rooted in ancient Christianity and paganism alike and that each *Wort* with the plural *Worte* is freighted with both meanings, even if the later one generally dominates: 'bread', 'wine', 'body', 'soul', 'spirit', 'heaven', 'hell', 'earth', 'man', 'woman', 'flesh', 'angel', 'devil', 'human', 'animal', 'God'.—In Aleksandr Blok's poem 'Twelve', Christ strides through the blizzard before the Red Banner of the Twelve, the twelve Bolsheviks, the twelve apostles, Nekrasov's twelve Russian bandits, but none of this makes Blok, Trakl's contemporary, a Christian or a Bolshevik or a terrorist poet; he is merely mindful of our origins:

> Ahead of them—with bloody banner,
> Unseen within the blizzard's swirl,
> Safe from any bullet's harm,
> With gentle step, above the storm,

In the scattered, pearl-like snow,
Crowned with a wreath of roses white,
Ahead of them—goes Jesus Christ.[7]

The same twelve gather in a poem which Trakl wrote six
years before Blok's:

Mankind arrayed at the burning abyss,
The roll of drums, dark warriors' brows,
Strides in a fog of blood, black iron's hiss,
Dejection, night in sad brains now:
Here's Eve's shadow, the hunt, and coin's red
    kiss,
Massed clouds, light breaks, the sacrament.
A gentle silence dwells in wine and bread
And gathered here are those twelve men.
Asleep beneath the olive trees they cry out in
    dread;
Saint Thomas sinks his hand into the bloody
    rent.

These twelve are the apostles, who could doubt it;
however, the twelve can also be us, and St Thomas is
among us too.

Incidentally, this poem was not written during the
war, as is often believed, but in 1912. And instead of
arguing about the extent to which it indicates Trakl's
Christian consciousness, it would be far more productive
to ponder how far his poem diverges from the scriptures,
in which the examination of Christ's wounds takes place
not on the Mount of Olives, the night of his arrest but,

according to John, eight days after his resurrection in a house with shut doors, shut for fear of spies and persecutors, and with eleven men, not twelve—one, Judas Iscariot by name, had hanged himself upon receiving thirty pieces of silver for betraying his master. *Coin's red kiss*, even among the *twelve*. The poetic simultaneity of three moments of the Passion does not just bespeak the presence of all history in each reader's time, it also fuses the two five-line halves of this ten-line poem in that unity of antitheses that is not a montage of starkly separate opposites but, rather, the unity of contradiction: *one* poem of *one* humanity, with each person both its part and its whole, albeit on different scales.—One of the twelve betrayed his master; the other denied him three times before the cock crew, and even the most faithful apostle slept.

A Christian message, certainly, but *only* that?—It seems futile to argue the point, for this pigeonholing does not exhaust the possibilities of the poem, does not even open it up. *A gentle silence dwells in wine and bread*— did the reader see this 'dwells'?—Rather than rely on labels, merely registering banalities and revelling in 'aha!' moments, it is far better to approach Trakl's poems by beholding his images: here, his message would be that of a silence that dwells.—Can the reader see it?—German has the image of silence or stillness reigning—hearing this, we inevitably see a throne room, or perhaps an assembly room, and on the dais a gaunt or possibly bloated figure in black Spanish court dress who has just stamped his foot and yelled for everyone to hold their tongues, and a grovelling crowd no longer dares to breathe: silence reigns.—And so does law and order reign.—'Deathly silence terrible' is what Goethe called the ultimate degree of such a silence. Life knows other kinds as well, and we find it highly instructive that in German when silence is spoken of, the image of power appears.—For Trakl, silence dwells, in many a place in his verses, *in black treetops—in empty windows—in the woods—in blue rooms*; and childhood, too, dwells thus in his poems, *quietly . . . / In a blue cave*; or the mysterious foundling Kaspar Hauser, *Earnest . . . in the shade of the tree*. Indeed, Trakl grants the attribute of dwelling even to the reigning powers: *Crystalline voice in which God's icy breath dwells*, speaking of Karl Kraus. And in 'Grodek' the spheres of reigning and of silence as an image of dwelling merge to form a prodigious mythos of the twentieth century's second decade: *But silent in the willow vale— / Red clouds in which a wrathful god dwells— / The spilt blood gathers*—here the twelve of Georg Trakl meet the twelve of Aleksandr Blok.— 'Dwelling' is an exquisitely mythical word; it speaks of abiding in a place where one's innate being can unfold (that one may have to spend one's life in an unloved place is another matter), and it is an exquisitely fraternal word, suffused with the breath of a community in which the right to self can be realized only as respect for that of others. In 'dwelling' dwells peace, even for the warrior:

That Roland the hero dwells on his horse, as the epic says, signifies a relationship other than master and servant; the words of the mystic Henry Suso, 'that a wolf shall dwell with a sheep', quiver with the yearning for a lost paradise. Johann Fischart observes, 'odd and churlish they must be / for no one cares to dwell near them'.— Where silence dwells, it does not wish to reign, it does not wish to silence others, it only desires a place to be.— Those unwilling to partake in its essence may avoid it; those who wish to partake may draw near and then words are spoken, if need be, there can be music too, whispers, sounds, even noise if necessary, all but one thing: compulsion.

A Christian message?—Hardly one for zealots, but Christians may settle that among themselves. Trakl's verse remains what it is: poetry of many meanings, belonging to all who strive for it.

Even the most difficult images open up once you manage to see them, though the sight does not fully exhaust them: inner space that no footsteps can measure. —With Trakl they are simple images of a simple life, which makes them hard to grasp today; their reality has grown unreal to us; and we seek in the symbolic realm things that were once in plain view: *Herdsmen buried the sun in the bare woods*, there are the herdsmen in the woods as winter nears, standing around a stone-lined fire pit, embers fading. *A fisherman / With a net of hair drew the moon from the freezing pond*—night fishing, the

moon reflected in the fishes' silver scales, or over the
empty net that is glimpsed beneath the pond's surface. *In
blue crystal / The pale one dwells*—in the blue of the sky;
in the mountains and even in the foothills one can see its
crystalline structure.—Beyond that, the 'blue crystal' is
infinitely more things, including the inescapable shining
cell of the *I* and the cell to which E. T. A. Hoffmann's
witch condemns her victims with the words, 'Into the
crystal!' But first of all, the sky is the sky, provided one
is able to see it. In blue crystal the pale one dwells, *his
cheek resting on his stars; / Or he bows his head in
purple sleep.*—On *his* stars, do we remember?—Will it
help readers to tell them that the first line of this poem,
'Rest and Silence', once took the following form, *The red
sun rests in the dead woods*; that the image of the net of
hair began like this, *A black bird sinks from a sky of hair*,
and that the sphere of dwelling first loomed as follows,
*A slender animal appears. In ancient blue / The striding
figure dwells, that once in dark waters / rested its white
cheek on purple fish*—fish which in a second draft
became *serpents* and in the third version *flickering
stars*?—Readers may be helped by seeing the natural
image; let them be helped by intuiting more of the
mystery at work in each line of poetry: the mystery of
creation and the mystery of meaning, always one step
ahead of understanding, growing still deeper as more and
more sense is revealed.—The appearance of the herdsmen makes the natural image clearer, but now Bethlehem
enters the verse: Christian poetry?—Ah, if only the angel

of St Augustine would appear before all hasty inter-preters, seeking to empty the sea with a seashell, just as the church father did with a mythologem.

Readers will need to remain mindful of mystery as the essence of all poetry, for we must now tell of our obsessive, protracted attempts to liquidate that mystery. —*Herdsmen buried the sun in the bare woods*: the sun is what no one can bury.

3.

J.N.Z., a guest lecturer in dialectical and historical materialism, whose lectures at the Soviet Union's anti-fascist schools for POWs—I graduated from one of them in 1948—our teachers heralded as the high point and which we students awaited in trepidation of scaling these heights, preferred, to our astonishment, to extemporize. With one hand in his trouser pocket he stood casually next to the lectern, bare even of notes, or strolled back and forth in front of it, in deliberate, Baltic-tinged German setting forth his thoughts—now on literature and art as a reflection of social life—with the confident ease of a cowboy unfurling his lasso, and he even had that hand motion: a nonchalant wave, then a toss into the distance and a gesture stiffening towards a goal.— Then his hand went back into his pocket.

Right away he had us spellbound: his chatty tone, jokes, anecdotes, dramatic tension; comparisons astonishing but understandable, drawn from our everyday experience; the audacious voicing of our most secret questions; and all the while, never assuming more than a modicum of background knowledge, he pressed ahead with his line of argument so single-mindedly that it gave us, the lost and confused, exactly what we needed: the stability of a direction leading out of the past.—I owe him a great deal and I mean that quite honestly.—He understood how to deal with us as none of the other teachers did; he spoke to us like an equal, cracking jokes yet aware of our worries, he voiced what we didn't dare think, and sometimes he made us laugh wholeheartedly, then fall silent in consternation: setting forth philosophy as a history of everyday life, in the midst of our mirth at his sprawling story he tied the thread to form an ethical conclusion no one could escape: in *this* laughter we were fascists still, and he exposed us.—His lectures were followed by suicides, and by profound happiness at the path discovered.—I felt that they gave meaning to my future life which after the devastating news of Auschwitz I had conceived as a rejection of everything to do with society. If ever, I'd thought as we trudged to work in the morning or thronged the clay stove in the evening, if ever again I should be so fortunate as to determine my own fate, I would dwell in the bowels of the earth, in a hole in the ruins of this Thebaid that was Germany, begging and subsisting on refuse, so as to owe the world nothing and incur no more blame: passing no judgements, giving no advice, taking no sides, harnessing myself to no cause, binding no one to me and fathering no child—a curse on all things with repercussions!—And believing no one any more, only my own senses.—In the infernal light of Auschwitz' fires this refusal of all action had seemed an unbeatably radical break from the entire past; now that I heard Marxist philosophy, I realized that this Diogenic dream merely inverted my previous notions of world dominion, a soiled coat turned inside out, and that the crucial break with the old had to mean breaking away to find the new, breaking down society to create an order that would forever prevent another Auschwitz: socialism even in Germany and even for me, son of a petty-bourgeois local Nazi leader, *Ortsgruppenleiter*. Breaks upon breaks, that seemed to be the price; but I remain committed to this insight, even if the vision of that hour no longer shines with such a pure light.

I had come to the school by some still-unclear coincidence; the reason may have been trivial, mixed-up names, human error, probably the instructions to send someone, anyone, and the randomly chosen shingle bore my name; the reason may have been trivial but the repercussions last past this day, a leap to a different life trajectory in a different society.—And yet the same thing happened to millions: a stroke across the map drew a border that parted not just human fates but also two peoples.—A vast subject, and I will resist the temptation to lose myself in it; suffice it to say that even now I recall my time at the school as the precious good fortune of a new beginning, when a process of transformation long unperceived in its many-strandedness (starting with the moment when capture by the Russians did not, as anticipated, mean death) forcefully entered the consciousness in surges of moral catharsis —albeit as the delusion of a goal already reached—as we gained a new communal spirit at the feet of the philosopher, moving from the fateful companionship of an accursed past and the whining companionship of the dismal present to the active companionship of humanity's dawn.—We, the accursed of the peoples. Then, all at once, I grasped the fairy tales: the hero, transformed into a wolf, is at last released from his spell.—After all, fairy tales are black and white.

These ideas that reached into our lives were not J.N.Z's own; he imparted, in his own way, the thought of Marx, Engels, Lenin and Stalin (or, to be precise, ideas of Marx, Engels and Lenin in the form that Stalin gave them). He offered them as though they were the sum of our experience, and grasping the teachings of these classic thinkers as something meant 'for us', with our very first insights we gained a simple-minded sense of understanding everything. 'Social determination', 'class character', 'the economic root', 'the superstructure determined by the base', 'the class standpoint', 'the class consciousness' —these distillations of sweeping mental and experiential processes became algorithms for us to solve the most complex problems in no time, for no problem could be too multifaceted to be swiftly reduced to linearity, to a dual coordinate system in which social classifications clearly determined all values, especially the moral ones. The world fell into black and white; it was 'all perfectly simple', to use a phrase still popular today, so everything in his lessons was perfectly simple—philosophy lessons, on quality and quantity, on contradictions, on God and matter, on being and consciousness, on the four main features of dialectics, on the laws of nature and the law of history, on the power of the masses and the role of the classes, and always lectures about ourselves. They were reductions of a very great philosophy to—well, at best, to what Hegel so emphatically warns against as 'edification'. We listened and listened.—He addressed us as 'comrades', lately the norm at the school; the epithet could only seem unaccustomed and alien to me, but I took it as a sort of baptism and regard it even today, though long since forfeited, as an honorific title. It made us equals, not just teacher and pupils; all the same, it would have seemed unthinkable to ask J.N.Z. for personal advice in an ideological quandary (at the time I knew no other quandaries—or, rather, all quandaries merged into the ideological), just as unthinkable, incidentally, as discussing his lectures: despite the suppressed doubts and qualms which, with ever-astonishing clairvoyance, he flung in our faces as 'remnants of the Old', they were quite simply revelations, proclamations of eternal truth, transfixing us in the sudden certainty that alternatives were unthinkable.—After all, the path we had finally found was the alternative to our accursed past, so—this seemed logical—all alternatives to this alternative could only ever be the Old, liberation from which, mentally and otherwise, was our most urgent desire.

This completely dualistic picture of the world (which, it is superfluous to stress, unduly distorted the teachings it invoked) was *precisely herein* a counterpart to the worldview which had formerly dominated our thinking, but it passed itself off as a complete break with the Old, and the only possible break at that. This contradiction remained stalled within itself, but as the mind chafed in its grasp without managing to discern it, it began to fester beneath the surface of the consciousness and in it festered Trakl's poem.

The city's white walls ring for ever . . .

The fractures stood out starkly; continua went long unnoticed, seeming the epitome of the unthinkable. And yet continuity lies in the person as such: the one transformed remains himself also; *also*, that is all, but also nonetheless.—Rather than leading from thesis and antithesis to synthesis, the stalled contradiction chased us in a circle: once the leap had been made, that is, once you had recognized the reprehensibility of what was known for short as 'the Old', no further development was possible, except to rigorously obliterate 'the Old' when it cropped up in your own sphere, and the object of the ultimate rigor was your own body. I see the man from the neighbouring cot hanging one morning from the joist of the latrine with a sign around his neck: I WAS A WAR CRIMINAL . . . We experienced in our own hearts what J.N.Z. proved to have been unfolding for thousands of years as the essence of all human history: the life-and-death struggle between old and new, reaction and progress, slavery and liberation: *Mankind arrayed at*

the burning abyss, and after Auschwitz this abyss burnt
only within.—A tormenting thought: Was there no third
way? This constantly suppressed question, startling me
with goblin-like malice in my most confident moments,
why, it too could stem only from the 'Old', from those
foul, muddy, tenaciously clinging vestiges which J.N.Z.
kept exposing within us, sometimes sharply, even harshly,
but usually with the understanding smile of one who had
been through it before us, for he was not afraid to admit
that he had suffered similar tribulations. In his lecture on
the necessity of atheism he explained that he knew from
his own torments of conscience what it meant to free
oneself from the quagmire of traditional thought, but his
example showed that it was possible and how: through
unflinching faith in the sacred goals, relentless ideological
toughening, tireless vigilance, unblinking self-criticism
and, above all, the unconditional devotion of the little *I*
to the worldwide community of struggle with the Great
Stalin at its forefront, a community to which we too
could belong one day, just as he, once its foe, now
belonged.

We gazed at him: an everyday figure, stocky, a bit
stout, badly fitting suit, massive nose, powerful shoulders, sparkling blue eyes, jaunty hair; we'd never have
guessed at the pastor, we'd have liked to believe he was
a cowboy.—But he was a professor of philosophy, and
now that he spoke unasked, as though reading our
thoughts, on the question of a 'third way', he became the

professor in appearance as well: now, for the first and last time, he stood behind the lectern, both hands raised adjuringly, exclaiming to the auditorium with the solemnity of one announcing a truth of faith: '*Tertium non datur*! There is and can be no third way!'—These, by the way, were the only foreign words he felt he should inflict upon us; he traced them back to the law of the excluded third, likewise the only figure of logic he showed us.— His translation was correct, even with the addendum; however, the same cannot be said of the connection he drew: this law was one thing, ideological and political alternatives another. But J.N.Z. expected no background knowledge on our part, only false consciousness, and his success bore him out.—*Tertium non datur*.

I can't go into detail here either; I will confine myself to the outcome: that we grasped the most complex thing as 'perfectly simple'. The battlefront between reactionism and progress ran through the millennia of human history, demanding a clear 'for' or 'against' in every sphere of social activity, in art and literature too, for now he was speaking of Marxist aesthetics and, he said smiling, some of the—now he smiled no longer but spoke with thoughtful forbearance, his hand sliding from his pocket—some of the academics sitting before him, those with philosophical backgrounds, so to speak, would surely ask why his course failed to discuss the 'Beautiful' or the 'Sublime', or suchlike. Having said 'or suchlike', he was smiling again, not mockingly, not even pityingly, just cockily, a boyish, triumphant smile, and it made everyone certain of understanding aesthetics as well now, just as they had understood dialectics and materialism.—A wave of the hand; he paced up and down.—It was all perfectly simple.

'All right, then, the Beautiful,' he said with a smile: Certainly reactionary aesthetic thought took this very seriously, the Beautiful in Plato, the Beautiful in Kant, the Beautiful in empirio-criticism, there were entire libraries about it, tomes running thousands of pages in which many an academic right here in this auditorium had no doubt immersed himself once, but—we were still laughing when in a switch to devastating seriousness he stopped smiling and his hand pointed back over our heads into the recent past—but had this knowledge stopped him from fighting for fascism, the ugliest thing in the world? No, it hadn't! And why not? Was it because he was stupid? No, not because he was stupid but because he had relied on those particular formulae, and those formulae had been created solely to be relied upon by the reactionaries. Not one of them served progress! Not only had the educated academic's knowledge not enabled him to recognize the ugliest thing in the world, it had actually obstructed this recognition. For what was the meaning of 'beautiful', of 'ugly'? For a fascist, a burning Russian village was as a beautiful a picture as a muzhik's flogged back for a boyar, but the peasant and the Red Army soldier saw these sights with different eyes!

The same sight—now foul, now fair—all at once I grasped the witches in 'Macbeth': the heath soughs, the woods march, the murderers wash their bloody hands, and trembling with agitation I heard the teacher say that the ovens of Auschwitz had boasted the shape of Grecian temples and rosebushes had stirred in the breeze around them, a beautiful sight in bourgeois aesthetic terms, and from a vast distance I heard the teacher pose Gorky's question: 'On which side are you, masters of culture?'— I was no master, not even an apprentice—could I ask myself this question?—The teacher invoked millennia of history, and always the same barricade and always it had two sides: On which side are you, masters of culture? With the slaveholders or the slaves, the landowners or the serfs, the capitalists or the proletariat, the stokers of the ovens of Auschwitz or those who put out their fires?—The heath soughed; fair was foul, foul suddenly fair: I saw the factories of my childhood, desolate walls, smashed panes behind which cogwheels and drive belts shrieked; nestled in the leather armchair in the dining room I saw the grey processions through the morning gloom, tin flasks on belts, shoulders drawn up, wrapped in hatred and contempt; again I felt myself shudder at the sight of this alien grey world and shuddered most at what I and my childhood home had been: those club chairs in SS-black; that faecal-yellow hussar jacket with death's heads and whipcords; that kissing of hands— swine slobbering; those shammed compliments—wolves panting; those table conversations—rats squeaking; the fine china we ate from, the crystal glasses we drank from—the ghastly banquet of the dead. And now I saw the dawn on those faces I'd never seen as faces before.—Could I become one of them, I, son of the *Ortsgruppenleiter* and factory owner, would the class of the future admit me? I desired it with all my heart, I desired to fall in with their procession, on my belt a tin flask that now seemed beautiful, as beautiful as everything from this class I yearned to belong to, and suddenly all the terms I had first heard here at this school, which had alienated me like a strange jargon, seized me with magical force: 'class', 'class struggle', 'revolution', 'trade union', 'proletariat'; and I fell hardest for those whose very form proclaimed their otherness: 'prodprocess', 'orgbureau', 'diamat', 'Sovnarkom'.

Fair was foul and foul was fair; and I heard my teacher explain that these values, too, were class terms, evolved from class experience, shaped by class interests, determined by a class standpoint, and this class standpoint was what we always had to ascertain, in each book, in each film, in each song, each play, indeed each meaningful phenomenon; *that* was the essence of truly scientific aesthetics and once we had grasped it, we would hold the key to all the spheres of art and literature which bourgeois academics in their ivory towers loved to romanticize as 'full of mystery'; as everywhere, their sole interest was to obfuscate the truth, the truth that was perfectly simple when regarded from the class standpoint.

I vividly recall that at these words I was overcome by the same emotion as on arriving at the foot of the Caucasus, or actually a sort of counter-emotion: whereas then, in the shattered harbour, I faced the continent of the Other, the unknown into which fate bore me as the bird Roc bore Sindbad, now I was standing on a summit, at my feet a long-familiar realm I'd once wandered as in a dream, in rapt wonder, through castles and cities that lay open in their mystery and that now, from my great height, I seemed to see in their class character and thus to grasp completely. A presumptuous delusion; to me it seemed science. And there is a twofold sacrilege I am aware of only today, though I know quite well that the seed of this awareness was planted together with the hubris and that I felt this beginning as well, as a piercing, inexplicable shudder.—One sacrilege or, rather, one side of my sacrilege mocked the mystery of poetry while the other mocked social experience. On the latter let me say at least this much: class consciousness, if the word is to retain its meaning, cannot be replaced by two or three trivial ideological formulae and no cheap propaganda lecture can teach anyone a class standpoint.

By cultivating this presumption, I now believe, that doctrine unmasked itself. I did not come from the working class, had never taken part in its struggles, never seen a factory from the inside, never joined a union: what arrogance to speak, after two weeks, of a 'class standpoint', as though that were a station you could buy a ticket for! That must have been where the shudder came in: it entered my consciousness as a moment of astonishment and as the sudden certainty of coming up against an existential problem that was far from being mastered simply by possessing a formula.—But there wasn't even a formula, I don't recall the least attempt to define terms such as 'class consciousness' or 'class standpoint'; it was simply assumed that everyone had them at their command if they'd learnt their lessons and knew all the quotes by heart.

Back during my initiation I had no time to think about it further, for J.N.Z. now took a practical example to elaborate what it meant to distinguish between 'beautiful' and 'ugly' from the class standpoint. We should recall, if we pleased, that just a short time ago we'd zealously sung: 'We'll go marching onward 'til all's smashed to smithereens!'—Had we sung it zealously?—Yes, we'd sung it zealously.—Had it seemed like a beautiful song?—Yes, it had seemed like a beautiful song.—But what was being propagated in the form of this song? The destruction of the entire world, meaning the destruction of socialism too! And what did the young folk sing today in that part of Germany where the people enjoyed true freedom? 'Build up, build up, Free German Youth, build up!' And what was going to be built? A better future, for a better life, the anti-fascist democratic society which, when the people wished it, would one day evolve into socialism! Was any formula needed to determine which song was beautiful and which was ugly? And at that we'd already struck up the beautiful one.—He sang along at the top of his voice, legs spread wide, keeping time with his raised arms, and then—I'll summarize here—he took children's books everyone had read, operettas everyone had heard, films everyone had seen, so as to demonstrate the different methodologies (though I believe that expression was not yet in vogue and he used the word 'instruments') by which the ideologists of reaction influenced the people with their cultural barbarism: the open propagation of such inhuman goals as war, anti-Sovietism and racial fanaticism; the use of superficial diversions and moral corrosion to distract the masses from their true interests; finally, the most dangerous method of all, and the hardest to see through: a critique of various isolated phenomena of capitalism in its decline, one which was often ostensibly radical but, rather than showing the way out, drew from these evils no conclusion but despair, paralysing the masses and preventing them from getting to the root of *all* evils— the relations of production! These critiques might dazzle the eye with their sophisticated techniques, they might confuse the mind with their feints, but if you approached them from the class standpoint, you quickly discovered that they preached nothing but—if we'd pardon his saying so—the 'ultimate wisdom' of the eternal philistine: the world is wicked, mankind is wicked, let's weep and moan, there's nothing else we can do about it!—*Under oak trees we sway on a silver barge.*—J.N.Z. slammed his fist down on the lectern: 'But there *is* something we can do, comrades, that's the crucial thing—the world can be changed!'

With this blow of the fist, I grasped everything.—It smashed a mental block behind which one vestige of the old lay entrenched, the scales fell from my eyes and the teacher's words voiced my thoughts: Enough of that hypocrisy! Down with those vile books that wallow in lamentation and sorrow and heartache, with exquisitely turned phrases whining about this grievance or that, and only helping to perpetuate them! Down with all mystery, down with mysticism and murk! Let the bourgeoisie lap it up, let the reactionaries praise the darkness, let the dead bury their dead, we'd fall in with onward-striding life!—Had J.N.Z. said that, or was it a voice within me? Thinking about it today, I believe it was the teacher; I would have used the phrase 'revolutionary life'.—I felt as though it were morning, the world lay flooded in light and I strode to meet it, in line at last in the proper rank and file.

My fellow students must have felt the same, and our teacher seemed to sense how his words moved the listeners. No more blows of the fist, no mockery, no sauntering; right hand outstretched above our heads, he took stock with compelling calm: If it was right (and it was) that the new always seems imperfect when compared with the old, yet has the future on its side; and if it was right (and it was) that the cultural superstructure moves in accord with its social base, growing, blossoming and declining along with it as the old is forced into the grave by the new, then it was impossible not to conclude that even the formally weakest work of a young socialist culture towered above that of the bourgeoisie. For this work showed the way out of *all* afflictions, even the despair and helplessness felt in the struggle to create a new society in which art and literature too, developing in a state of true freedom, would be raised to undreamt-of heights, radiating their beauty before the working people!

The bell rang; J.N.Z. had mastered the art of ending his lectures so that the last syllable coincided with the first ring (though sometimes he scorned it and far exceeded his time). The bell rang; there was thunderous clapping and stamping and J.N.Z. nodded to us as he left: modest, smiling, almost abashed by the storm of applause that demonstrated our understanding of aesthetics.

Psalm
dedicated to Karl Kraus

There is a light, extinguished by the wind.
There is a moorland inn, where a drunk man sets
  out late one day.
There is a vineyard, burnt and black with holes
  full of spiders.
There is a room, and they've whitewashed it with
  milk.

The madman has died. There is an island in the
    South Sea,
To receive the god of the sun. The drums strike
    up.
The men perform warlike dances.
The women sway their hips in twining vines and
    fire-flowers
When the sea sings. O our lost paradise.

The nymphs have abandoned the golden woods.
The stranger is buried. Then a glimmer-rain
    begins.
The son of Pan appears in the shape of a
    ditch-digger,
Sleeping through the noon on the smouldering
    asphalt.
There are little girls in a yard in dresses of heart-
    rending poverty!
There are rooms, filled with chords and sonatas.
There are shadows, embracing in front of a
    mirror that's gone blind.
At the hospital windows convalescents warm
    themselves.
A white steamer on the canal carries bloody
    contagions upstream.

The strange sister reappears in someone's evil
    dreams.

Resting in the hazels, she is playing with his
stars.

The student, perhaps a doppelganger, gazes after
her from the window.

His dead brother stands behind him, or walks
down the old spiral stairs.

In the darkness of brown chestnuts the novice's
pale form fades.

The garden's in the evening. In the cloisters the
bats flutter this way and that.

The caretaker's children stop playing and seek
the heavens' gold.

Last chords of a quartet. The little blind girl
walks trembling down the lane,

And later her shadow gropes along cold walls,
amid fairy tales and sacred legends.

There is an empty boat, drifting in the evening
down the black canal.

In the gloom of the old asylum human ruins
decay.

The dead orphans lie against the garden wall.

From grey rooms step angels with faeces-stained
wings.

Worms drip from their yellowed eyelids.

The square where the church stands is sombre
and mute, as in the days of childhood.

On silver soles former lives slip past

And the shades of the damned descend to the
sighing waters.
In his grave the white magician is playing with
his serpents.

Mute above the place of the skull, God's golden
eyes open.

The reader may welcome some factual information to supplement our personal experience with Trakl's 'Psalm'. —The Psalms are sacred songs of the Jewish congregation; there are one hundred and fifty of them, making up a book of their own in the Old Testament, the Book of Psalms.—Johann Gottfried Herder called them an 'ocean of one hundred and fifty songs', and their unsurpassable translator Martin Luther extolled that ocean's inexhaustibility:

> Where are finer words of gladness than in the Psalms of Praise and Thanksgiving? There thou lookest into the hearts of all the saints as into fair and pleasant gardens, yea, as into the heavens, and seest what fine, hearty, pleasant flowers spring up therein, in all manner of fair gladsome thoughts of God and his benefits. And again, where wilt thou find deeper, more plaintive, more sorrowful words of grief than in the Psalms of Complaint? There thou lookest again into the hearts of all the saints, as into death, yea, as into hell. How they are filled with darkness and gloom by reason of the wrath of God! So also, when

they discourse of fear and hope, they use such words, that no painter could so portray [. . .] thou shalt therein find thine own self, and the right 'know thyself'; God himself also and all his creatures.[8]

The Psalms are prayers in song form, eruptions of words from the individual or the people, impelled by a beleaguering abundance of feelings, heartrendingly joyful or heartcrushingly painful, for when the heart overfloweth, the lips do as well, you must speak to survive and so you speak to God in the congregation.—By far most of the psalms are psalms of complaint, outcries from amid the everyday woes that course through this people's centuries, as constant as the tides: war, captivity, enslavement, injustice, oppression, persecution, mockery, sickness, plagues, natural catastrophes, despair and the crushing sense that it bore the blame for its own afflictions, for its sins. In his sadly forgotten book *The Spirit of Hebrew Poetry*, Herder traces back the characteristic form of these poems, known as parallelism, to their essence, the compulsion to speak:

> So soon as the heart gives way to its emotions, wave follows upon wave, and that is parallelism. The heart is never exhausted, it has for ever something new to say. So soon as the first wave has passed away, or broken itself upon the rocks, the second swells again and returns as before. This pulsation of nature, this breathing of emotion, appears in all the language of passion . . . [9]

'Parallelism' denotes a long line formed by two half-lines intimately joined by affirmative repetition, by the introduction of a new, modifying aspect, by an addition that creates a higher unity, or by juxtaposition, contradiction.

Perhaps we had best acquaint ourselves with one psalm in its entirety; here is Psalm 80:

> Give ear, O Shepherd of Israel, thou that leadest
> Joseph like a flock;
> thou that dwellest between the cherubims, shine
> forth.
> Before Ephraim and Benjamin and Manasseh
> stir up thy strength, and come and save us.
> Turn us again, O God,
> and cause thy face to shine; and we shall be
> saved.
> O Lord God of hosts, how long wilt thou be
> angry
> against the prayer of thy people?
> Thou feedest them with the bread of tears;
> and givest them tears to drink in great measure.
> Thou makest us a strife unto our neighbours:
> and our enemies laugh among themselves.
> Turn us again, O God of hosts,
> and cause thy face to shine; and we shall be
> saved.
> Thou hast brought a vine out of Egypt:

thou hast cast out the heathen, and planted it.
Thou preparedst room before it, and didst cause
    it to take deep root,
and it filled the land.
The hills were covered with the shadow of it,
and the boughs thereof were like the goodly
    cedars.
She sent out her boughs unto the sea,
and her branches unto the river.

Why hast thou then broken down her hedges,
so that all they which pass by the way do pluck
    her?
The boar out of the wood doth waste it,
and the wild beast of the field doth devour it.
Return, we beseech thee, O God of hosts: look
    down from heaven,
and behold, and visit this vine;
And the vineyard which thy right hand hath
    planted,
and the branch that thou madest strong for
    thyself.
It is burnt with fire, it is cut down:
they perish at the rebuke of thy countenance.
Let thy hand be upon the man of thy right hand,
upon the son of man whom thou madest strong
    for thyself.
So will not we go back from thee:

quicken us, and we will call upon thy name.
Turn us again, O Lord God of hosts,
cause thy face to shine; and we shall be saved.

Trakl is an Austrian, for him the vineyard is everyday life, not a piece of exotic scenery. It would be pointless to ponder whether or to what extent Trakl arrived at the structure of his 'Psalm' by studying the Book of Psalms; such a method would be foreign to him. But it might help readers to know that the first version of 'Psalm' ends with the words: *How vain it all is*!— This line is unquestionably a citation from a different part of the Old Testament, from the book 'The Preacher Solomon' ('Qoheleth' or 'Ecclesiastes'), an almost maniacally bitter reflection on transience that comes again and again to the realization: 'All is vanity and a striving after wind'.—'All' is all that is earthly, except death, and 'vanity' means both 'puffed up' and 'trifling'.

How vain it all is!—This quote in the first version of the 'Psalm' seems contrived; it is clearly meant to act as a keystone, joining the lines to form a vault, but stands as a foreign body, dissipating rather than focusing. Trakl was not the *poeta doctus* type, the learned poet whose work references his great predecessors and foregrounds this referentiality.—Of course all poetry is a web of referentiality, working with words that are freighted with meaning and thus with references. The title 'Psalm' is a reference, as is a similar title, 'De profundis'. '*De profundis ad te clamavi Domine*', 'Out of the depths have I cried unto thee, O Lord', is the beginning of another psalm (Psalm 130 which is so often set to music), but this point of departure, the cry from the depths of affliction, is virtually the only commonality with Trakl's poem.— Despite its opening words, Psalm 130 is a psalm of hope: 'For with the Lord there is mercy, / and with him is plenteous redemption.' Trakl's 'De profundis', by contrast, is a poem that leaves no hope at all, not even that of suicide.—Here the contradiction is not a correspondence; no compositional, intellectual or artistic relationships can be detected; the Biblical words that proliferate in 'De profundis' are equally elements of Trakl's daily life (the thorn bush, the gleaning orphan, the well, God's silence, the angel) and their shared spirit of truth is not a reference, it reflects their common place in the primeval element of all great poetry. But whereas the psalms cry out from amid an affliction which was apparent to the speakers, which they and their brothers experienced first hand, so that it did not need to be named explicitly ('foes' stands for any real foe), Trakl speaks out to a world which does not share his underlying emotion, which thinks itself intact, well-appointed, firmly rooted, unshaken, and all this only heightened in the prognosis for the future: 'I shall lead you to glorious times!'; two flashing eyes and a flashing sword.—And the exultant applause of the sated ten thousand.—That is the false collective consciousness against which Trakl's psalms, stark and implacable, make their existential declarations:

There is a field of stubble, where a black rain falls.
There is a brown tree, standing all alone.
There is a whisper-wind, circling empty huts.
There is a light, extinguished by the wind.
There is a moorland inn, where a drunk man sets out late one day.
There is a vineyard, burnt and black with holes full of spiders.
There is a room, and they've whitewashed it with milk.
There are little girls in a yard in dresses of heart-rending poverty!
There are shadows, embracing in front of a mirror that's gone blind.
There is an empty boat, drifting in the evening down the black canal.
From grey rooms step angels with faeces-stained wings.

And the grey rooms are the same rooms of which he wrote:

There are rooms, filled with chords and sonatas.

Israel's psalm-singers saw the scorched vineyard before them; Trakl's time gleamed with golden wine and his day's song, its true psalm, was warbled in Franz Lehár's *The Merry Widow*, the cultural sensation of the time.— Trakl, the great carouser and pub-goer, was never aloof from robust pleasures—*The small inn appears on the wanderer's way. / Sublime is the taste of nuts and young wine. / Sublime: to reel drunk through the darkening woods*—but the drunk man who sets out from the moorland inn late in the day in 'Psalm' is drunk in a different way: in him, wine's delight turns to wretchedness, like the milk defiled as whitewash.

But we do see one correspondence between the 'Psalm' and the psalms: the formal element of the long line, departing from the usual form of Trakl's stanzas, and the attendant parallelism, though this manifests itself more in the stanzas than in the individual lines. No doubt the reader has noticed that Trakl's 'Psalm' falls into four equal blocks of nine lines apiece, concluding with one single line, a true keystone now in this second version. The first version has the same structure: four stanzas of nine long lines and then a single last line, though here it does not act as a keystone.

The first stanza of the 'Psalm', in the second version and the almost identical first version (the ninth line contains an exclamation point which was later deleted: *O! our lost paradise*), begins by revoking creation or, rather, reversing it. The book to which the psalms belong opens with the words of creation, 'Let there be light!', whereas Trakl's 'Psalm' begins with the reversal: *There is a light, extinguished by the wind.*—Not brightness and warmth but darkness and soot, a striving after wind: here it extinguishes the light.—These four lines of reversal are followed by four lines of what the poem calls a 'lost paradise': *There is an island in the South Sea, / To receive the god of the sun. The drums strike up. / The men perform warlike dances. / The women sway their hips in twining vines and fire-flowers / When the sea sings.*—The images of a lost paradise *here* and one *yonder* that is not lost form an antithetical parallelism, but between the opposing blocks comes the half-line: *The madman has died*—who is this madman?—Before substantiating our answer, which is that we cannot know, let us examine the other stanzas for structural parallels that may help us.

The second stanza, consistently set *here*, shifts from the present tense to the past, extending the yearning gaze towards far-off places to become a gaze into past times: *The nymphs have abandoned the golden woods.* This broadens the *yonder* and *here* of the first stanza into a *once* and a *now*, so that an intuition of loss glimmers in the generations of the present, in sequences of images almost entirely external, recognizable today on a stroll through Trakl's city: the courtyards, the rooms, the mirrors, the hospital, the convalescents, the canal and even its blood. And once again a foreign body, but this time in the very second line: *The stranger is buried.* —Who is this stranger? Is he the madman?—Possibly, we do not know, does the poet?—We do not know that either.—The third block of verse confronts a dream with everyday reality; here the foreign body is a student's dead brother, once again a stranger. Then, in the fourth stanza (in which, now emphatic parallelism, all is blighted, dead: *an empty boat*; *human ruins*; *the dead orphans*; *angels with faeces-stained wings*; *former lives*; *shades of the damned*) there comes, in conclusion, the enigmatic interjection: *In his grave the white magician is playing with his serpents.*—That silent frieze of dead men that runs through the poem: *the madman*; *the stranger, the student's dead brother, the white magician with his serpents*—who are they?—A silent frieze of dead men that runs through the poem. That is all we know.—Are we satisfied?

We are never satisfied.

What can we do?

One apparent way to assuage our desire for understanding would be to search Trakl's *oeuvre* and find where else and in what contexts a word such as 'madman' or 'magician', or an image constellation such as 'plays with serpents' occurs, in the hopes that these new perspectives will enlighten us. However useless this method would be were it based on the tacit assumption that those *Worte* are *Wörter*, that is, each with only one unchanging meaning, it does seem likely to help if we grasp the words as *Worte* and in the spirit of Baudelaire: 'To divine the soul of a poet . . . look for the word or words that recur in his work with most frequency. They will betray his obsession.'[10]

Here are the results, which the reader may verify: *the madman*, unless we have missed something, appears nowhere else in Trakl's work, nor does the same noun with the indefinite article; but the word 'madness' appears as many as twenty times. *And what is golden and true is oft revealed to gentle madness* ('Spot by the Woods'); *Of God's colours dreams the brow, / The gentle wings of madness feels* ('Whispered into the Afternoon'); *O, the madness of the city* ('To Those Now Silent'); *Flags of scarlet, laughter, madness, trumpets* ('Trumpets'); *Darkly madness sings in the village* ('Play Fragment I'); *But as I descended the cliff path, madness seized me* ('Revelation and Downfall'); *Where of old the holy brother walked, / Sunk in the gentle strains of his madness* ('Helian'); *So that dark madness sank from the sleeper's brow in spasms* ('Sebastian Dreaming'); *For ever more radiant from black minutes of madness / The patient one awakes on the petrified threshold* ('Song of the Departed')—we could cite all these passages, yet none of them, for all their echoes, tells us for certain who *the madman*, whose death stands as a caesura between the *now* and the *once*, actually is.

The word 'magician' appears twice, each time defined in a way that at first glance raises our hopes. In the poem 'Evening Muse', the first line of the third stanza is: *The soul listens gladly to the white magician's fairy tales* (so the adjective 'white' appears here too). Moreover, the third line of the quatrain entitled 'Karl Kraus' is: *Wrathful magician*, and Karl Kraus, the man addressed here, is also the dedicatee of Trakl's 'Psalm'.—Does this get us anywhere?—The line from 'Evening Muse' seems clear and comprehensible; there the magician is a storyteller. But it is impossible to tell whether 'white' is a description of clothing or skin colour, or a vestige of the term 'white magic'—that is, the art of salutary, benevolent sorcery as opposed to the baleful black arts—and there is no apparent reference to a grave or to serpents. Besides, 'white' could well be a euphemism; the 'white magician' might be a drug—or drugs as such. And as for the quatrain that evokes the Kraus dedication, not only do the attributes differ (*Beneath whose flaming mantle the warrior's blue armour rings*), it is simply an embarrassing notion, unworthy of Trakl, that the magician in the 'Psalm' could be Karl Kraus in person.

All that leaves us with is the 'playing with the serpents'. In a posthumous complex of poem fragments, we find the following stanza: *Where in dark rooms the lovers once slept / The blind man plays with silver serpents, / With the moon's autumnal melancholy*. Much here echoes the 'Psalm'; now the reader will sense, as is often claimed, that all Trakl's poems are ultimately one single poem in ceaseless variations, with verses, images and words that flow into and unfold from one another, that have freighted one another, in the shifting recurrence of ever-different sameness, with the utmost degree of meaning and mystery. We could cite Stéphane Mallarmé or T. S. Eliot or Attila József or František Halas to prove the same thing for modern poetry in general, but still this does not tell the reader who *the madman* is supposed to be: indeed, the more these new perspectives seem to illuminate, the more obscure the mystery grows.

Perhaps we must accept the assessment made by Hugo Friedrich in his famous work *The Structure of Modern Poetry*, which we have studied gratefully and with profit, despite its one-sided insistence on obscurity:

> Modern poetry compels language to take on the paradoxical task of simultaneously expressing and concealing a meaning. Obscurity has become the predominant aesthetic principle, outlawing the customary communicative function of language and letting the poem hover in such a way that it withdraws rather than comes closer. [. . .] Obscure poetry tells of events, creatures or objects without informing the reader of their cause, their time or their place.[11]

The reader may concur with these analytical words—while qualifying their claim to absolute validity—but the problem is far from being solved. His urge to *understand nonetheless* grows stronger and stronger—just who is this *madman*, damn it, there's got to be an answer!—and helplessly his gaze turns to scholarship. Here it may help readers to know that before arriving at the above conclusion, Friedrich reflects on the use of the definite article in modern poetry by citing the example of a poem by Gottfried Benn, in which the equivalent of *the madman* is 'the pearl'; in this variation too, the question and the answer remain the same: 'What sort of a pearl does Benn mean?'—'We do not know'.

Let us listen to Friedrich again:

> In normal usage, the definite article defines, points out, an object that is known or has been previously mentioned. It linguistically confirms what is known [. . .]. In modern poetry, however, the definite article is used in such a way that, as a determining means, it elicits attention, which it then instantly disorients by introducing an entirely new object. This practice, as well as the similar use of other determinants such as personal pronouns, adverbs of place, etc., was employed by nineteenth-century poets, especially Rimbaud. In our century this practice has been spreading immoderately, becoming a chief stylistic feature.[12]

And the paragraph before this says of the distinction between the definite and indefinite article: 'The object named by the noun, the pearl, was not anticipated by anything; and, because the definite article coincides with this unfamiliarity, the pearl is vague and mysterious. The *in*definite article ("*a* white pearl . . .") would have evoked a different atmosphere.'[13]

The same is true of Trakl:

There is a light, extinguished by the wind.
There is a moorland inn, where a drunk man sets
out late one day.
There is a vineyard, burnt and black with holes
full of spiders.
There is a room, and they've whitewashed it with
milk.
A *madman has died. There is an island in the*
South Sea . . .

—The poem is spoilt; anecdote, not mystery, the verse verges on the absurd.

In the lines that go before, '*There is*' lends solidity to the '*a*'.—We will resist the temptation to hold forth on the use of the definite article to denote singular things or types (not necessarily identical with *familiar* things). Pursuing Friedrich's train of thought, we interpret readers' urge to understand as an unacknowledged jealousy towards the person who must surely know who 'the pearl' and who '*the madman*' is, namely, the poet who wrote these obscure verses. Whether the poet really knows it is beyond determination, but the definite article makes readers feel certain that he does, and it is this that goads them on to wrest forth the solution to the riddle: they would gladly let the interpreter put the poet to the rack and force the answer from him.—For what in truth is always hidden in the obscurity of great poetry, namely, mysteries of human existence, here presents itself to the reader as a riddle, and a riddle in contrast to a mystery is that which utterly loses its essence once its solution—always unambiguous, that is, expressible in *Wörter*—is known, while a mystery persists no matter how thoroughly it is illuminated.—'Guess what this is: / Sat a bird featherless / on a tree leafless / came a lady mouthless / ate the bird featherless'—this is the snow, consumed by the sun, and once the solution is given, the riddle, as a riddle, is gone; yet the mystery of the white snow remains a mystery of deadly purity and beauty, the cold that warms, the crystalline fragility that entombs a valley with a thunder as loud as its floating from the sky is silent, and is then drunk by Lady Mouthless.—This mystery, if one embraces it, grows deeper the more it is explained, the more openly it lies before us: it is outward because it is inward while a riddle is only outward.—Part of the curse of modern poetry (here 'modern' denotes an epoch, such as 'archaic' or 'gothic' or 'baroque') is that the mystery in its verses too often presents itself first as a riddle, thus paving the way for charlatans: their hermetized trivialities are given the chance to seem profound, obscure and enigmatic, though often they do not even pose a riddle: 'Guess what this is!'—a mere striving after wind.—It takes long or intuitive experience to distinguish the darkness of a crystal from the darkness of the secretion with which a squid cloaks itself in camouflage; this stubbornly acquired experience is the transit duty that modernity demands and Trakl's readers, too, must pay it, but they will do so only if they sense that the investment will be worth it.

There is a light, extinguished by the wind—whoever feels affected by this line must venture down alone into the darkness that entombs the *madman*'s death. Adopting others' opinions is useless, indeed harmful, if the starting point is not this affect, though at first you cannot say what touches you and why this concerns you. You sense that this is your affair, and now of course you want to understand *everything*, understand it for certain and all the way through, you want the mystery to be solved like a riddle, for it presents itself in riddling fashion; but the denial of this solution is precisely what lends these poems their goad.—Without this goad Trakl's 'Psalm' would not exist and would not be what it is, and this is what makes it the antithesis of its archetype the Biblical psalm, in which everything must necessarily be understandable.—That quality of light, that different crystalline substance, cannot be recaptured by an act of will today: *O our lost paradise!* The Bible's psalms refresh the thirsty; today's arouse an unquenchable craving, doubly goaded by the mystery behind the riddle and by the ultimately inescapable compulsion to think that a solution must exist, though there can be nothing but interpretations, including—perhaps—the author's own. But the interpretations are of the mystery; a riddle cannot be interpreted, only solved, and its proposed solution can be false or true; *tertium non datur*, here these words are fitting.

And so readers have everything to gain by taking the supposed riddle as a mere passageway into the mystery of the poem, venturing their own interpretation instead of awaiting the solution with bated breath; they are too timid to do so as long as they fear that it might not be correct, not identical with the sole solution which only an expert can deliver—*De profundis ad te clamavi Domine*! We don't mean these words ironically; we are all too familiar with the despair of drowning in the tantalizing quackery of trivial intelligibility, able to grasp a yearned-for message just well enough to conclude that it may be meant for us but we are not meant for it. And so we wait for an arbiter. But waiting like this for the opening of a door, you block yourself off from the open: a parable by Kafka. That the poem affects you means precisely that it opens towards you, but this very act of opening points into a darkness that appears as a closed door.—Step in, instead of waiting for the key; nothing is blocked off here, but walking in the dark can trip you up as well. Readers must accept that the obscurity of certain modern poetry is a non-negotiable part of its essence and that without it Trakl's poems would never be what they are, not only in form (if I may sunder conceptually what cannot be sundered materially) but also in content—they could not be said differently, not even a single word; they are not the translation of something that could be said simply into something of arbitrary difficulty.—Their darkness stands before bright light, just as the midnight blue and black of a cathedral window glows forth as darkness only against the sun. —Otherwise it would not be recognizable as darkness.

Readers must start from the premise that an understanding of Trakl's poems can be achieved not by postulating some bindingly conclusive, bindingly unambiguous and evidentially deducible authorial idea and reconstructing it, but only through an act of secondary creation, through their own interpretation.—And so you could replace *the madman* with whatever you like? —Not with whatever you like; rather, with whatever the poem dictates.—But what it dictates is dark!—Dark yet concrete, and deep within the light, bound up in a framework of words:

> *There is a light, extinguished by the wind.*
> *There is a moorland inn, where a drunk man sets*
>   *out late one day.*
> *There is a vineyard, burnt and black with holes*
>   *full of spiders.*
> *There is a room, and they've whitewashed it with*
>   *milk.*
> *The madman has died. There is an island in the*
>   *South Sea,*
> *To receive the god of the sun. The drums strike*
>   *up.*

The men perform warlike dances.
The women sway their hips in twining vines and
fire-flowers
When the sea sings. O our lost paradise.

Yes, we will give our interpretation of *the madman*. But first, let the angel step forward.

I no longer recall the East Berlin bookshop—back in 1950 there were countless used-book dealers—where I bought my first Trakl collection upon my release from war captivity. But I know it was the legendary first edition of a selection made by Franz Werfel and published in 1913 by *the* expressionist publisher, Kurt Wolff Verlag in Leipzig, simply entitled *Poems* and comprising Volumes 7 and 8 of the series *Der jüngste Tag* [Judgement Day], that the booklet cost f50 pfennigs and lay in a cardboard box full of tattered pamphlets and that when I picked it up, the faeces-stained angel was suddenly standing outside on the rubble heaps.—He looked at me; I gave a start and he was gone; the sun shone on the sooty bricks that stank of rats and carrion, and I walked home as in a dream and read.

An utterly different Trakl spoke forth from that slender black paperback with its title set in a square of algae green: a lovely city, sunny silence, ancient squares spun in blue and gold, young mothers at flower-filled windows, a gleam of fire, purple, enchanted maids and: *The son of Pan appears in the shape of a ditch-digger, /*

Sleeping through the noon on the smouldering asphalt. *—A red that, dreamlike, agitates you.*—I read and read.—And the conversation with my father, not five years past, rose dreamlike from my memory, flooded with mild moonlight, and I gazed, moved, at the man in the yellow hussar jacket and tasted the wine I hadn't touched since.—He seemed so helpless now, leafing through his pharmaceutical books: now I saw his worn face; when I'd thought of him before, I had always seen his Nazi uniform.

But the strangest thing, I distinctly recall, was that I treated Trakl differently than all the other writers and poets whom I had read en masse and helter-skelter ever since returning from war captivity and taking a position as a cultural policy apparatchik. I had learnt to grasp these 'minstrels and bards'—words I now used ironically —solely as advocates and ideologues in the service of a social milieu or political force and ultimately of one of the great classes whose antagonism shapes society. I automatically ranked them this way, indeed I read them only to rank them, with unmistakeable signs to go by, such as reverence towards the throne and the altar, kowtowing before the upper class, castigating the lower, blindness towards the struggles of the masses, a lack of faith in social progress, an inward turn, doubt in the possibility of truly knowing the world and, above all, a failure to show the way out, a failure marking the great ideological divide of twentieth-century culture.—I marked such passages in the margins: red for approval, green for questions, brown for censure; this, I thought, was exhaustive understanding and historical materialism. —Exposure of the essence.—Everything else—formal questions, immersion in metaphors and, above all, subjective feelings—had to be trivial in contrast, indeed could only distract and confuse, and to engage with these things would mean evading the crucial question, that of social determination.

With Trakl I abandoned those notions; I simply rejoiced in his lovely, sonorous, benignly bright verses that painted in sounds and sang in hues, in bell-hues and garden-sounds, touched by the way the same words recurred as rhymes, so insistently circling a piece of dreamland:

> *Where you walk, autumn comes, and evening.*
> *Blue deer that under trees resounds.*
> *Lonely pond in the evening.*
>
> *Soft the flight of birds resounds,*
> *Sadness above the vaults of your eyes.*
> *Your slender smile resounds.*
>
> *God has bent your lids to vaults.*
> *At night stars seek, Good Friday child,*
> *The vault that is your brow.*

I read and read. Should I say that I felt a forbidden emotion? The poem teemed with signs marking it as aggressively anti-realist and its poet as petty bourgeois and pious!—That sweet, unadmitted *nonetheless* of taking pleasure in what was supposed to displease me —did it arise from the word-magic of melancholy and forlornness? It must have, and the darkness and dissonance in these verses must have had the same effect, impossible to ignore, but presumably I took it as a foil against which brightness could paint itself as brightness; the whole volume was composed that way. *Thus over the clouds I trace their journeys. / There—decay breathes soft and makes me shudder.*—Did I feel it; did I shudder?

All I know is that I read as though dreaming, then snapped the book shut and put it away and afterwards avoided discussing Trakl with my department head, who had been a young Nazi like me and had a biography much like mine but with three more years' experience both there and here. For that reason I often sought his advice, though sometimes I argued with him; we were both committed to methods of social classification, but he was much stricter than I in taking them to mean that whatever the feudal or petty-bourgeois artists and writers produced was the direct realization of an ideological mission, one that might be self-imposed, in certain exceptional cases, but whose stimulus was still predominantly material: they received money or privileges in exchange for translating precisely defined political content into a literary or artistic or philosophical form (or they did so in the hopes of such remuneration, though sometimes

they miscalculated and the powers that be proved stingy).
In short, they were nothing but agents and the only
approach we could take was to unmask them. Hardly a
nuanced aesthetic assessment: paid hacks and polemicists,
the lot of them!—A robust cutting-edge theorem. I no
longer recall exactly why I contradicted him: it was
true, I agreed, that every work of literature or art had
to be assessed ideologically and defined in terms of class,
that was unquestionably the key consideration; at the
same time, during the creative process someone might
be oblivious to the social content of his art or poetry or
philosophy; in the honest belief that he was merely
working poetically or philosophically he might produce
this or that ideology, but since he was simultaneously pro-
ducing it as art and philosophy, one could, indeed one
must also evaluate it as such and differentiate between
better and worse. The argument centred partly on Stefan
George and Nietzsche and expressionist paintings; I had
trouble imagining that the first two had pocketed fees
from Krupp and its syndicates to blaze an intellectual trail
for fascism, and that the painters had received a salary to
distract the masses from their struggle and besides, I
didn't think they were hacks.—My boss called me a
'mystificator' and an 'irrationalist' and accused me of
right-wing deviation and Freudianism in disguise; I took
this very seriously.—With Trakl, then, it was different; I
read in a state of dreamlike rapture, but suddenly this
act of pure reading somehow seemed unauthorized and
I stopped.

A little later, and once again I don't recall where, I bought a copy of *Sebastian Dreaming*, published in 1915 by Kurt Wolff Verlag. Trakl had held its proofs in his hands but did not live to see its publication, not that I knew this at the time; I knew nothing of the lives of the poets.—I wanted no image.—Nor do I recall when it dawned on me—probably intuited quite early, articulated very late—that in Trakl's poems the living is to the dead as evil is to good or, rather, as the debased is to the exalted, especially since his verses often show the living as dead and the dead as alive:

> *With the forms of dead heroes*
> *You fill, moon,*
> *The taciturn forests,*
> *Sickle moon—*
> *With the tender embrace*
> *Of the lovers,*
> *With the shades of fabled times,*
> *You fill the mouldering crags all around;*
> *How blue is the light*
> *That shines towards the city,*
> *Where cold and malign*
> *A rotting race dwells,*
> *Preparing their white grandchildren's*
> *Dark future.*

I could not have known that poem at the time, as it was not included in either of my two books; but in 'Night Romance', following the evocation of a dance of life uniting the decrepit, the mad, the sick, the murderous, the desperate, the sayers of prayers and the patrons of whorehouses, I had already seen the writing on the wall: *In basement vaults, by tallow light / The dead man draws, his hand so white, / A grinning silence on the wall.*—*The dead man*, once again; not 'a dead man'— here all the persons labelled with the definite article are types, representatives of their kind, a marionette tableau mechanically unwinding (only *lonely man* and *lovers* glide along outside it), and however often I read this poem, the dead man down there in the flickering light, drawing the sign of the times, is the only one who is truly alive. Or in the 'Lovely City'; looking closely, all that endured in the surface shimmer of darting impressions was this: *From within the brown-lit churches / Gaze death's unspoilt effigies, / Escutcheons of royalty, / Crowns a-glimmer in the churches.*—And in the landscape of the burnt vineyard and the milk-washed room, wasn't the first living man the one playing with his serpents in his grave: *the white magician*? And when it said: *The madman has died*—might not this death be a passage into life, into the lost paradise?—Questions I certainly did not ask; at the time I took such poems merely as dreams; they did not enter my reflections, nor did the grave and the magician enter my consciousness.

The poems I did reflect on were entirely part of a daily routine and this routine denied all irrationality. It, and I, found fulfilment in education campaigns, lectures at indoctrination seminars, discussions of current issues, political teleology. The poems I favoured were ones needed for this routine, ones showing a way out of our difficulties, positive stanzas, constructive verses that gave strength and inspired confidence and—extolling the Good already achieved and pointing to the still-to-be-achieved Even Better (the comparative form was a poetics unto itself)—could be declaimed as a garnish for lectures, or, themselves garnished by music, at ceremonies: mobilizing, arguing, filling with enthusiasm. Viewed in this light, dreams were welcome too, as visions of the future sprung from a faith that was knowledge: 'Distant bliss that shines up close', as Johannes R. Becher put it in a poem.—Trakl was unsuited for the purpose, but as Becher's name shows, these useful poems included creations of a high order: odes by Pablo Neruda, satires by Erich Weinert, Vítězslav Nezval's 'Song of Peace' and, above all, the poems of Vladimir Mayakovsky in which even the route of a streetcar could serve as a topical argument: 'Different is its route today / To socialism all the way!'—Mingled with them was the flimsiest of doggerel, including most of what I wrote (late in the evenings, true to childhood habit), such as a 'Sunday of Rebuilding', with the eschatological conclusion: 'Towns and people, rivers and land / we shall shape with our young hands / To bring the epoch of ruins / and war to an end.'—This felt good and right to me, and apart from warning me not to write that sort of thing during working hours, my department head had few objections; these verses were clearly and unambiguously partisan—'unmistakeable', as people still say today, though the unmistakeable quality was not a poet's subjective singularity but, rather, the clarity of the message in the sense of political norms, that is, the fact that such unmistakeable poems consisted of *Wörter* rather than *Worte*. However, my poems contained other things that critics deplored: apart from the mythological references, they chiefly found fault with wrongly applied colours that failed to correspond with natural phenomena, or that were even ascribed to abstractions which, after all, could only be thought of as colourless, 'black curses', for example, or 'bluely blaring flights' and other unintelligible things that contradicted the principles of realism and popular accessibility. In this connection my boss was fond of the expression 'understanding at the first go': a poem, the critics demanded as well, had to be 'understandable at the first go'.—I took this seriously too and tried my hardest.

I no longer thought of Trakl now, and for the moment the angel did not reappear; I was wrapped up in routine which was completely of this world and consumed me to the point of exhaustion.—So did my writing.—At the time I didn't dream of becoming a writer, though I often wrote through the night after work, kept awake by an excess of tea, cigarettes and alcohol.—Poetry, says Baudelaire, works like fate.—But daily routine worked the same way.

Before sharing our interpretation of the *madman*'s death or, rather, our associations with this passage, we would like to point out a stylistic principle of Trakl which readers have surely noticed, one which Trakl himself describes in a letter to his friend Erhard Buschbeck:

> Yesterday, after explaining at length that his work was kin to mine, etc., Herr Ullmann read me a poem and lo and behold, it turned out to be more than merely kin to my poem 'The Stormy Evening'. Not only were specific images and turns of phrase borrowed nearly verbatim (the dust dancing in the gutters, clouds as a flight of wild horses, windows rattle at the rain's thrusts, all glittering the sudden rainstorm, etc.), even some of the stanzas' rhymes and their significances are exactly the same as mine, there is my exact same visual style of using a stanza's four lines to forge four individual visual components into one single impression; in a word, the raiment, the hard-won style of my work has been reproduced down to the tiniest detail.

Readers can easily find examples of this stylistic principle in many of Trakl's poems, the self-contained lines tending to end with a full stop; the 'Psalm' is also constructed this way.—Trakl continues:

> Though this 'kindred' poem lacks the vital fever that had to create precisely this form and though the whole thing strikes me as soulless and shoddy—as a complete unknown, one whose

voice goes unheard, I cannot help caring that I
might soon see the caricature of my own face
held up as a mask before a stranger's!

Like most of Trakl's letters, this one gives us no place
or date; scholars (there is a treatise on the question) date
it back to the second half of July 1910, when Trakl had
published only three or four pieces of juvenilia in local
newspapers. He was not known beyond this local readership until 1912, when his works appeared in Ludwig von
Ficker's monthly *Der Brenner*, which Karl Kraus extolled
in his own literary journal *Die Fackel*: 'The fact that
Austria's only honest journal appears in Innsbruck ought
to be known, if not in Austria, at least in Germany, whose
only honest journal likewise appears in Innsbruck.'—
Alas, to this day it is hardly known at all.—As for Trakl's
insistence on the uniqueness of his formal principle,
literary scholarship informs us that he did not invent
these sequences of self-contained lines with stand-alone
images; they were emblematic of the poetry of that
time, beginning with Detlev von Liliencron's poem 'In a
Big City'.

Detlev von Liliencron, 'In a Big City'

Past me drifts in the city's sea
This man, then that, one after the other.
A glance into the eyes, already past.
The organ-grinder grinds his song.

Past me drips into Nothing's sea
This man, then that, one after the other.
A glance at his coffin, already past.
The organ-grinder grinds his song.

A funeral march floats through the city's sea
Crossing people's paths, one after the other.
A glance at my coffin, already past.
The organ-grinder grinds his song.

True, this work does not quite strike us as demonstrating that formal principle but, rather, one of its existential premises (it seems to us that Liliencron's poetic 'I' produces and represents the coherence which Trakl's poem rigorously obliterates); however, we offer several other examples by Liliencron's contemporaries to illustrate the theory:

Alfred Lichtenstein, 'Twilight'

A pudgy boy plays with a pond.
The wind's got caught up in a tree.
The sky looks dissolute and wan,
Its rouge applied too sparingly.

Bent aslant on their long canes
They cross the field, two gabbing cronies.
A blond-locked poet just might go insane.
A fine lady trips up a pony.

Stuck to the pane—a fat man's snoot.
A lad calls on a wench soft and fair.

A grey clown pulls on his boots.
A perambulator shrieks, dogs swear.

*

Jakob van Hoddis, 'World's End'

The philistine's hat whirls off before his eyes,
The airs resound as though with screams,
Workers plummet from the roofs and smash to
    smithereens,
And along the coast, we read, the tides are on the
    rise.

The storm has come, the wild seas bound
Ashore to rush through all the breaches.
The sniffles seem to be going around.
The trains are tumbling from the bridges.

*

Georg Heym, 'Bastille'

A forest of sharpened scythes entrenched.
The Rue Antoine is blue and red
With multitudes. Their brows are set
With white-hot rage. Their fists are clenched.

The tower looms dead into the sullen skies.
From tiny windows wafts its icy dread.
From the lofty roof, where watchmen tread,
The cannons' iron gullets terrorize.

A door creaks. From the Tower's black wall
The envoys emerge, all dressed in black,
And mutely wave. They'll be no use at all.

Paris is raging, it rises to fight back.
With knives and clubs they brave the cannon-
    balls.
The Tower shudders under their attack.

*

Georg Trakl, 'The Stormy Evening'

O the scarlet evening hours!
Flickering at the open window
Vine-leaves wound into the azure
Harbour fear's ghosts in their tangle.

Dust dances in the gutter's stenches.
Windows rattle at the wind's thrusts.
Lightning drives on lurid cloudbanks
As a flight of wild horses.

The fishpond's mirror shatters loudly.
Round the window gulls are shrieking.
A blazing rider clears the hilltop
To smash to flames against the fir-tree.

The sick cry out in hospital.
The night's blue plumage whirs and ruffles.

All glittering the sudden rainstorm
Thunders down upon the rooftops.

Yet what Trakl's letter asserts is not so much originality
per se as the validity of his original. He accuses Ludwig
Ullmann not just of copying him but also of copying him
soullessly: the imitator *lacks the vital fever that had to
create precisely this form.* That is a subjective criterion;
what objective form could it take? What sort of bond
universally seen as binding ('form') could take four (or
in Trakl's case usually three) images that seem separate
and randomly arranged into a stanza and nonetheless
forge [them] into one single impression such that readers
receive this impression as well? What touchstone would
they have to test it with? That the poet acts on an inner
compulsion which he then sees validated means nothing
in itself; all writers subjectively claim that their work is
obsessive and their intentions are successfully realized
(and God knows they assert it all the more vehemently
the more amateurish their efforts are). But what would
be a binding standard? Trakl himself does not propose
one; does he trust the reader to tell the difference
between the 'good' original and the 'bad' copy, between
the *face* and the *mask*? He does not seem entirely certain
of that, for his letter continues:

> *Truly, I am revolted by the thought of under-*
> *going assiduous journalistic exploitation even*
> *before I enter this paper world, I am revolted by*
> *this gutter of mendacity and meanness and all I*

can do is bar my door and house against all this
spawn of fog. For the rest, I shall be silent. All
the best from your G. Trakl.

Incidentally, Trakl and Ullmann were soon recon-
ciled; the outcome of the affair is not terribly important,
but the matter at stake is articulated here with unusual
trenchancy and devastating frankness: authenticity and
inauthenticity in modernism, the living and the dead, the
face and the mask, obsession and assiduity.—The fact
that this problem arouses Trakl's revulsion against poetry
in general shows the position to which life relegates it.—
At nineteen, Trakl's favourite poet, Rimbaud, leapt from
the 'paper world' into an explosion of life which he
squandered in North Africa, while Trakl entertained desperate plans of entering the colonial service in Borneo—
I am revolted by this gutter filled with mendacity and
meanness. The history of modernism is a history of the
ruin of its creators.—*The madman has died*—doesn't it
sound like a release? And at the same time so horribly
cold.

However tempting it might be to take a closer theo-
retical look at the stylistic device of the poetic montage,
for that is what Trakl is using, we will confine ourselves
to our experience, which tells us that to illuminate problems of poetry, it can help to postulate an analogy
between poems and dreams.—'Dreams are involuntary
poetry,' says Jean Paul (citing Kant who in turn belongs
to a tradition of ancient insight) and the montage of

disparate elements is a dream principle par excellence. All readers are familiar with a certain dream experience: occurrences or figures which in everyday life one would experience as unrelated, which one could not imagine brought together even by chance (a sewing machine and a jellyfish, for example) nonetheless manifest such a strange mutual affinity that even when the individual components appear separately in time and space, they are immediately recalled as a whole, sparking a sensation that is more than perplexity: fear, frisson, delight, dread, desire.—Psychologists believe that despite their disparate appearance, elements thus related stem from a shared root that is not visible in everyday life, though that is where it is ultimately found.

Trakl, in his letter, claims an analogous feat: to join heterogeneous things, isolated lines of verse, to form a homogeneous stanza; that is, to evoke their commonality. With regard to 'The Stormy Evening', the vehemence of his claim startles us, for we do not even perceive the images' asserted heterogeneity: their unity is provided by the theme; the sequence of the lines follows the unfolding of a natural process, and after more than half a century's reading experience, something which Trakl's contemporaries must have found astonishing and striking seems familiar to us. And we have long viewed the Impressionists' canvasses as classics, indeed as venerably conventional: landscapes by Erich Heckel and Ludwig Kirchner serve as postcard motifs; Surrealist devices on

advertising posters solicit the attention which they themselves, long familiar, barely attract any more—yet contemporaries regarded such creations as an outrageous
bedlam of paint blotches or visual monads, lacking all
discernible meaning. Nowadays we are inclined to take
'The Stormy Evening', in all its words and images and in
its temporal sequence, as something almost documen-
tary; yet the 'Psalm' makes us ponder, even today. *There
is a light, extinguished by the wind. / There is a moorland
inn, where a drunk man sets out late one day. / There is
a vineyard, burnt and black with holes full of spiders. /
There is a room, and they've whitewashed it with milk.
/ The madman has died. There is an island in the South
Sea*—readers will acknowledge the disparate nature of
the images, but will they acknowledge the necessity of
their sequential arrangement as a coherent stanza? By
asking who *the madman* is, they show that they do not;
reading 'The Stormy Evening', no one would think of
asking what rain bursts in upon the last stanza: *All glittering the sudden rainstorm / Thunders down upon the
rooftops.* It is the rain that follows the thunder, in the
poem as in the reality that the poem identifiably reflects.

But what reality does the 'Psalm' reflect, or, put differently: By what logic does the death of the madman
come between a room whitewashed with milk and an
island in the South Sea preparing to receive the god of
the sun? What necessity unites the isolated images, and
if it cannot be found in some verifiable external reality,
natural or historical or social, what specifiable inner

necessity would it be, what substrate of the poetic imagination whose faithful reproduction—this is still the reader asking—could serve as the criterion for poetic success? Our conception of understanding poetry is so crucially shaped by theories of reproduction that they influence our poetic experience as well: the more a poem moves us, the more urgent our attempt to comprehend it rationally, or, rather, to resolve it into something purely rational by grasping it as a reproduction to be traced back to a supposed original; this rationalization would entail naming the congruities and incongruities between the secondary and primary aspects, and their causes and their consequences.—To this end we locate the poem in a natural context or in the historical time of its creation and if we cannot find an external congruity there, or in an artwork that has verifiably influenced our poet (or at least could have), we seek it in the author's intent, in his consciousness which we imagine deducible and objectifiable. We lose sight of our affect, yet it is precisely the objective criterion we so desperately seek. It is the element that raises a poem above its existence as a specific poetic genre—that is, as a construct of poetic diction—an existence defined in purely formal terms, recognizable and diagnosable at a glance, and makes this poem into a work of art, achieving what Trakl feared was impossible, that is, distinguishing the living face from the mask. Of course this criterion is *also* subjective, but only from our point of view; from the perspective of the poem it is completely objective, taking the poet's subjective will to homogeneity and elevating it into a fact of artistic success. In this qualitative sense, a poem does not become a poem because it fulfils certain formal rules, but because a reader constitutes it. Until then it merely appears to belong to the genre of poetry, a dead form, interesting only once the interest in the poem as an artwork awakens.

This reader may take decades or even a century to appear, but if he does not, the poem does not come into being as poetry: there is no objective poetic form that legitimizes something a priori as a poem in the sense of an artwork.

This is not a subjective criterion, though a poem's objective character stems entirely from the subjective. Poems are a different kind of dream, but while someone else's dream tends to bore us, however it may have stirred up the dreamer (which is why he shares it in search of sympathy), a stranger's poem can move us so greatly that even when it remains obscure, we feel that it belongs to us and, what is more, that something belonging to us has been revealed for the first time through this poem: This too is ours! or: But this *is* what is ours, we just didn't know it, at most we intuited it!—However, this peculiar fact must mean that what stems from a certain root in the poet points to a root in us, the readers, that we share with him, the primal ground that brought forth and nourished both his root and ours: A collective subconscious? —So many questions, and each answer only leads to more questions.

This question, for example: if we say that being affected by a poem is an experience of the *tua res agitur* ['This is your affair'], why is there still so much we fail to understand; why, in the case of the 'Psalm', do we still have no idea who *the madman* really is? How can something be 'ours' that in rational terms we don't have at all?— Here we could reply that 'having' need not be identical with 'having in rational terms': if you suddenly feel that someone is yours, you need not know why that is. But this answer fails to satisfy us. It cannot, for the thing itself is tormenting, and its torment lies in the contradiction that for every inch by which we convert poetry into rationality, we both approach the poem and leave it behind while the same is true for every inch by which we fail to convert it. The more the poem's mystery besets us, the more it becomes ours, for it besets us from within; but in the process it also becomes more and more an Other, a magical force from the outside world before which we stand helpless, and this helplessness in turn goads on our will to conquer the poem through comprehension. —What maddens us most is that this escalation, by constantly yielding new facets, shows us more and more urgently that it is in fact our affair.

And another thought alarms the reader. If it is he who makes a poem into a poem, what prevents him from making a bad decision that would inevitably reflect back upon him? Not only does the reader constitute the poem, it constitutes him in equal measure: in this act he reveals himself. He defines himself with his decision—what if he were to constitute something that in the view of certified experts did not deserve to be called a 'poem', if he were to champion the wrong thing, thus proving himself the sort of person who champions the wrong thing! Mere ridicule would be bad enough, but there can be other consequences as well. Perturbed, the reader casts about— where is the touchstone for testing 'false' and 'authentic', or, in more common terms: 'false' and 'correct'? How can you reliably tell a 'true' poem? What criteria are available, what distinguishes the poet from the charlatan and bestows upon the reader the certificate of proper discernment?

Do these questions sound familiar? Here too they express the distress of perplexity: What *ought to* affect the reader? Or as a blunted and thus more acceptable question: What *ought* he to like?—The reader is in genuine distress: But there must, he cries in despair, there *must* be some yardstick of values that can objectify my choice!—There are many, dear reader, not just one, and that's the thing! They are touted daily, they compete with one another, sometimes within one and the same aesthetic, and so the question of the yardstick and criterion for an artwork shifts to the question of the measure for the normative power of such a yardstick, the criterion of authenticity for the criteria by which authenticity is determined. What determines the constitutive value of an artwork and what determines the determination of the determiner? Truth?—But what is truth?—The faithful reproduction of realities?—But what is reality and what is its reproduction? Ideological correctness? Social utility?—But what is ideology and which of the many ideologies is the right one; and what use is poetry to society?

To state the sum of our experience: the reader must learn at last to trust himself. His affect *is* the criterion determining that for him this poem is a poem; there is no longer such a thing as an authoritative canon.—There never was, or there always was, yet the poems that claimed a place in world literature were often those that shattered a canon that had previously expelled them as monstrosities.—The reader must learn at last that his affect is *his* affect, and he is affected by a poem, not by its conformity with a rule or a body of ideas. With his affect the reader confronts the poem all alone: that he can share his affect with others, that with this choice of his he often joins a community of the likewise affected that does command a yardstick of rankings and a catalogue of examples, and that he pits himself against a community with an opposing hierarchy, is a different and secondary matter. The progress of one's experience as a reader, the influence of criticism, honing one's taste, cementing or modifying one's opinion—sometimes to the point of rejecting it—all these are consequences and conclusions; the first thing is affect.—And what if one is affected by kitsch or 'the wrong thing' or 'a harmful thing'? Let others be the judge of that, and judge they will; perhaps some day one will second their opinion, but for the person affected, poetry is first of all that which affects him, and he is affected by it if he professes it to be his own—even if only to himself. Generally by stating that he likes it; will he stand by what is his? Will a derisive look suffice to make him abandon it? And what does such a look scrutinize and measure: the degree of affect or strength of character, the poem or its reader?

There is no objective criterion for poetry, but the affect says that the reader has something in common with the poem, and this thing in common is experience. This is the homogeneous element of all poetry, that densest freight of human experience in the smallest of spaces: words, metaphors, lines, stanzas; and facing it is the reader's experience, demanding words to voice itself to him, and when these two things converge, the lack of words and the force of words, the reader, in an ever-new act of creation, constitutes this verbal construct as poetry and himself as its co-creator. Those who do not go through this, and be it with kitsch (through which something older acts, the kernel of poetry, the shard of myth from which even denatured things ultimately stem)— those who never go through this will never know a poem as experience; for them it will always be a heterogeneous thing, bringing neither delight nor torment. The poem of little concern to the reader does not reach into his being, which is not to say that it does not concern him at all and that he does not wish it to be within his reach: as a source for the literary history buff, as edification for the assiduous, as an ideological vehicle for the political militant, as an object on which to demonstrate the exaltation or rejection of that which the poem represents. Such people can perfectly well get their opinions out of reference books and align them with the critics of the day; they'll spare themselves, and the poem, a great deal.—For poetry works like fate.—But daily routine works the same way.

> But do you think then the gods have opened
> The doors and made the way joyful in vain?
> That for nothing the kind ones have bestowed
>   on the banquet's
> Great fullness not only wine, but berries and
>   honey and fruit?
> And given the red-purple light to the songs of
>   the feast,
> And the night cool and calm for deeper con-
>   versing with friends?
> If you ponder more serious things, save them for
>   winter,
> And if you're looking to marry, be patient, for
>   May will bring lovers their day.
> Now, though, we need something different, come
>   now and honor
> The fall's ancient rite, since the noble one still
>   blooms with us.

For today only one thing's important, the fatherland,
And everyone offers the festival flame what is
his.

[. . .]

You angels of the fatherland, O you before
whom a man by himself
Will find his eyes failing no matter how strong,
and his knees broken,
And he'll need all his friends for support and
must ask
For his dear ones to help him to carry his burden
of joy,
Accept my thanks, O kind ones, for him and for
everyone else
Who make up my life and my wealth among
mortals.[14]

Hölderlin's 'angel of the fatherland'—does it surprise
the reader to encounter him?—I knew as much about
Hölderlin as any Nazi schoolboy and I had him in my
knapsack as well: 'You've come, O battle! The youths are
already flowing—'and 'For the righteous slay as if in a
spell, / And the songs of their fatherland / Weaken the
knees of those without honour',[15] and: 'Live, O
Fatherland, remain there on high / And don't count the
dead! O my belovèd, / Not one too many has died for
you '[16]—I was all the more astonished that even after the

destruction of what we had once deemed the fatherland and what then made us curse patriotism, I should meet Hölderlin once again, in these verses and in new ones that went still further.—But it was not my boss (I won't mention him again) who encouraged me to rediscover Hölderlin—the man who invoked anew this singer of the fatherland had an authority second to none, for he was not just a poet of great stature; his life, which carried far more weight for me, seemed exemplary.

The biography and work of Johannes R. Becher entered my life belatedly, when I was a POW. In some strange way, his verses took things that had burnt out and turned to ash, and restored them, not so much with a glimmer of old splendour and a breath of old warmth as with the possibility of renewal, indeed with the possibility that being burnt out and burnt down was what allowed them to become themselves at last—Germany, the Germans, their history, their vilified, vaunted character, their cathedrals, their woodcuts, their symphonies and songs, their poetry, their philosophy, and the dreams and torments of all these things' creators—as though the pure ore of essence could flow only from the scorched earth left by Germany's defilers.—These poems promising the warmth of hope were themselves strangely cold; for all their assertions, they lacked a certain element of fraternity, but their theme bridged whatever distance their author built around them: a profession of faith in something that seemed utterly used up, however tormenting the need for it might still be.

What was happening at that time, moving the masses and, above all, the youth (usually with a strange insouciance, too, for all the deadly earnest one always sensed in Becher), is surely hard to grasp today; reclaiming political values by defiantly employing, in the name of revolutionary renewal, concepts abused to the point of being used up: 'the people', 'the fatherland', 'the future', 'the meaning of life', 'the common good', 'self-sacrifice', 'faith', 'mission', 'struggle', 'devotion'. Today these concepts have suffered a new sort of attrition, but back then they had begun to shine once again, rising like Lazarus, even such rejected words as 'heroism' and 'hero'.—Their resurrection took place under the banner of Truth. As Becher put it in one of his speeches:

> The term hero, too, must again be given true meaning and true heroism liberated from those who usurp the title of hero, or confer spurious titles. Only a people that refuses to fall for false heroes and that recognizes its true heroes will be capable of distinguishing truth from falsehood and will pursue truth as traced by the footsteps of those who, under the hardest of circumstances, have furnished such radiant proof of true heroism.

'True': a word with two meanings.—It became the most important word of its time, but was used almost only as an attribute not a predicate, applied not to statements but to concepts and their underlying socio-psychological realities: 'true belief', 'true freedom', 'true interests', 'true fatherland' and thus, too, 'true art' and 'true poetry'. —Not 'This reasoning is true', but 'This is the true reasoning'.—Thus the word revealed its origins in the arena of dynastic politics rather than the labours of cogitation; its antonym was not 'untrue' in the sense of incongruence with reality but, rather, 'false' in the sense of 'illegitimate'.—The adverbial form was 'truly': 'truly good', 'truly beautiful', even 'truly true'.—In keeping with its origins, the word nearly always attached itself to postulates that constituted definitions: 'true art must . . . ', 'a true poem has to . . . '—Discourse short-circuited to proclamation.—These aestheticians, invoking Marx, passed off their efforts as the 'true aesthetics' and thus— giving the attribute a gnoseological twist—as the 'only scientific aesthetics', a branch of the science of world transformation which seemed to be what the world needed. Even in the sphere of aesthetics, all normative demands were made and robustly realized under the banner of historical necessity, treated as indispensable for building the new society which Becher had welcomed back in 1917, in the first hour of its existence, and which now blossomed on German soil too, as the German people's true fatherland: 'From the ruins risen newly, to the future turned we stand', in the words of the national anthem.—These are memories I am telling, and they are dear to me.—Oh, angel of my fatherland, will you show yourself again as you once appeared to me?

What was at stake, then, was true poetry, and we understood this 'true' as the fundamental rejection of all the lies of our cursed past, taking it as a proof of truth, though far more than that it stood for social legitimacy or political utility (which, in turn, the postulate of partisanship required us to take as truth).—I am speaking of how I perceived it; there were different experiences, or different aspects of this experience, which departed from the aesthetic sphere, but these things, however close at hand, long remained remote from me. Or to put it more precisely, they went unexamined for too long, though close as they were they ought to have reached me.—Rumours of disciplinary actions and arrests, for example: I fended them off; where did they go? Busy criticizing my past, I barely noticed my evasion of the present, though that need not be the consequence of delving into yesterday.— I projected a promised future onto my everyday consciousness and grasped it as Today: distant bliss that shines up close! And at the same time I began to drink and write questions at night in my diary that I struck out in shame in the morning, for I felt they were the germs of doubts, disbelief that this new society, being truly new, had the power to fulfil the ideals it had promised to bring to life, the ideals in whose name it demanded sacrifices and which it all the more stridently decreed to be fulfilled the more starkly daily life gave the lie to them: the *true* fulfilment was a given and if reality did not accord with it, he who acknowledged this contrast reflected not reality, but false consciousness. He saw the 'Truth' not as 'true' but merely as not real, and that was just how the enemies of the new saw it.—It was complicated and yet 'perfectly simple', another favourite phrase of the day.—By this logic, the true reality lay in the future; to announce it today became the mission of the poets, and the visionaries of such Tomorrow-Todays were invoked as a 'true legacy' in a 'line of true tradition'—which, albeit one-dimensionally, pointed to an inheritance whose champions cannot be thanked enough for reminding us of its crucial importance. 'And when the spirit of truth reigns in our literature, and the spirit of liberty and justice, then literature shall become power and the rest of our shame and disgrace shall, not long from now, be expunged: For the righteous slay as if in a spell, / And the songs of their fatherland / Weaken the knees of those without honour' —that is quite right, and Becher said so in 1942, as Hitler's armies besieged Lenin- and Stalingrad and carried Hölderlin in their knapsacks and believed themselves the righteous who, as we'd seen for three years of Blitzkrieg, truly slew as if in a spell; and then, when those beaten by the righteous sought to abdicate all fatherlands and flee into a realm of pure intellect, Becher recalled these words of Hölderlin again and again: 'Do you think— / It should come / As it did then: / They sought to found / A kingdom of art. But in so doing / They neglected the fatherland, / And miserably / Did fairest Greece come to ruin . . . ' And from all this he drew the conclusion: ' . . .what the works and deeds of the dead point to is a great historical path into the future'.

Pondering the truth—/ Much pain; a line by Georg
Trakl.—Becher called one of his invocations of epochal
experiences 'A Commemoration of the Poets Who Died
For Germany's Freedom', concluding it with the avowal:
'Here I stand, I can do no other. I believe in the German
people . . . I believe in Germany . . . '

This was written in 1947; what part of these words
could one wish to take back?

But there was a consequence to these statements. If
a true legacy was to be cultivated, it had to be separated
from a false one; preparing the ground for new seed
meant rooting out the old weeds, and these weeds were
called decadence, and one of its exponents, named
explicitly alongside Alfred Mombert, Theodor Däubler
and Else Lasker-Schüler, was Georg Trakl.

The naming of him struck me like a whiplash, and
the welts still smart to this day.

Decadence, usually called by the general term 'for-
malism', or at least implicitly included in it, was the pro-
totype of the condemnable, as justified less by arguments
than by circumstantial evidence; it was enough to declare
that decadence, according to one of its most zealous oppo-
nents, took 'society's failed and uprooted members, the
outlandish and the ugly, the sick and the atypical' as its
subjects, even its heroes, and lacked 'uplifting, forward-
looking content'.—A death sentence.—It seems improper
to place the names of its executors next to that of Georg
Trakl, for they worked like Faust's lemurs, too often in

total obscurity, but one stood out in stature, a novelist of undisputed rank whose epopee on the Young Guard in the Soviet Union's heroic struggle had moved us deeply: Alexander Fadeyev. In his famous speech at the 1947 World Peace Congress in Wrocław, before the world's intellectual and moral elite, he equated decadence with fascism: 'German fascism needed beasts. And the American monopoly capitalists need beasts to achieve their plans of world domination. The reactionary literati, screenwriters, philosophers and artists serve their masters faithfully. They elevate the schizophrenics and narco-maniacs, the sadists and pimps, the provocateurs and monstrosities onto a pedestal.'

Of course, Fadeyev did not mention Trakl's name, but didn't his list of contemporary cultural barbarities include, in essence, the same identifying marks of deca-dence?—As for Eliot or Miller, whose names he did men-tion, I knew only a few belief-beggaring quotes (or, rather, paraphrases), apparently ranging from the asser-tion that there was no such thing as human beings, only straw-stuffed scarecrows, to the cynical claim that the greatest bliss a person could achieve was not the engage-ment in the struggle for progress but the voiding of a full bladder.—Though I had not seen these statements in context, I had no doubts as to their authenticity and I flinched to think of ranking Trakl alongside such people.—Did he and this Eliot person really belong together?—I simply couldn't believe it: wasn't one poem called 'The Lovely City'? Didn't another laud the work of the peasants? And wasn't a third an emphatic avowal of Truth?

Hesitant, I opened the slender black book and found my hopes abruptly dashed:

Beneath the stars a man alone
Walks the silent midnight ways.
The dreaming boy wakes in a daze,
His face decaying in the moon.

The idiot girl weeps wild-haired
Behind the staring window's grate.
And in the pond, adrift so sweet,
Most wondrous lovers pass in pairs.

The murderer in his cups smiles pale,
The sick are seized by fear of death.
The nun with lacerated flesh
Prays naked before Christ's travails.

Soft in her sleep the mother sings.
At night the child seems quite soothed,
Its gazing eyes all filled with truth.
Inside the whorehouse laughter rings.

In basement vaults, by tallow light
The dead man draws, his hand so white,
A grinning silence on the wall.
The sleeper whispers through it all.

'Night Romance', the poem I'd chanced upon: didn't it unite all the features of decadence? Society's failed and uprooted members, the outlandish, ugly, sick and atypical danced in ghastly circles with narcomaniacs, sadists, monstrosities and gangsters; schizophrenics appeared twice, in fact, and with laughter resounding from the whorehouse, the pimps couldn't be far!—*The murderer in his cups smiles pale*: what a romance!—But perhaps the title was meant ironically, the juxtaposition critically; and weren't the forces of decay opposed by the power of the lovers whose humanity is preserved? *And in the pond, adrift so sweet, / Most wondrous lovers pass in pairs*—at that I grasped the full force of this 'in' as a *Wort* with the plural *Worte*: *in the pond*, not 'on the pond' or 'over the pond'. Those drifting past in the pond were the dead, just like the man down in the basement vaults, writing on the wall; here 'in' meant enclosure, and now it leapt out at me: the idiot girl in the barred room and *in the moon* and *in the pond* and *in his cups* and *in her sleep* and *inside the whorehouse* and *in basement vaults*, they were all stuck in cells and all alone, all isolated from one another, alone in their delusions and fears, and the only person walking through the night was *a man alone*—if that wasn't decadence, what was, and if this message didn't render readers helpless in the face of reactionary machinations, what could?—But the child, the child! I thought desperately, weren't its eyes all filled with truth? And up sprang the question: Hadn't all of them been children once, the nun, the idiot girl, the murderer, the whores, their patrons and their protectors, weren't Eichmann and Goebbels once innocent children? Didn't Trakl invoke, with this very origin, the senselessness of all hope and action?—It seemed it was so.

And *this* appealed to me?—Impossible.—*The dead eyes of a satyr stray / Where shadows into darkness glide*, I read on the next page; didn't my eyes stray to my past in just the same way? I leafed through the book, perturbed by the very titles: *Evening's Melancholy—Winter Twilight—Dream of Evil—All Souls'—Melancholy—De profundis—The Rats—Dejection—Psalm—Nearness of Death—Decay—Human Misery—Night Song*—so it slipped along, from decay to derangement, from disintegration to downfall.—And my other hope dissolved as well: *From the stove comes the grimace of embers / And a swarm of flies is a-hum. / The maids are listening bashful and dumb / And the blood knocks at their temples. // And sometimes covetous gazes meet / When animal fumes fill the air. / A farmhand says a monotonous prayer . . .* Was that how this poet portrayed the working people, the allies of the working class, descendants of the heroes of the Peasants' War?—It did occur to me that Marx had spoken somewhere of the 'idiocy of rural life', but inhuman conditions were one thing and the people struggling against them were another—likewise capitalism was barbarism, but did this make the workers barbarians? To be sure— that is, I was sure, though I had just as little first-hand knowledge of the workers as I did of the peasants—to be sure, individual workers might succumb to barbarism, but that hardly made them typical, and even if some farmhands and maids might submit so utterly to their urges that their existence amounted to little more, the poet was obliged to overlook this animalistic stratum of humanity.

Indeed, as I realized only now: what crass eroticism and sexuality (at the time it was a precept of enlightenment to draw a sharp and moralistic distinction between the two) erupted in barely veiled symbols from all these dark verses: *As in a dream she's met by laughter; / And she reels into the forge, / Shrinking shy before his laughter / Like the hammer rough and hard . . . —Prick black thorn . . . — . . . at red breasts suck / Sunken lips, and in pools of caustic black / The sun-youth's humid curls glide . . . — . . . Monkess! close me in your darkness . . . — . . . And at night they rush out from red flurries . . . — . . . A black horse rears up prodigious; the maid's hyacinth locks / Snatch at the fervour of his purple nostrils . . . — . . . A blossoming effusion gently ebbs / And unborn things sustain their repose . . . — . . . Mignonette's scent; and a fervid sense / Of evil . . . — . . . Moistening it, a rosy drop of dew / Clings to the rosemary: the scent of graves flows forth . . . — . . . A nest of scarlet serpents rears / Sluggish in her stirring lap . . . — . . . Beneath dark firs / Two wolves mingled their blood / In a stony embrace . . . — . . . lust, when in the green summer garden he harmed the silent child . . . —Your body is a hyacinth /*

In which a monk dips waxen fingers—and that was addressed to a boy, *To the Boy Elis*, which meant sheer pederasty, and as the line before that was *O, how long, Elis, have you been dead*, it meant necrophilia as well; and the defilement of a child; and sadism; and sodomy; and masochism; and masturbation; a compendium of perversions missing from Fadeyev's list, and didn't lines such as: *Siblings in the park glimpse each other trembling . . . — . . . Sister, your two brows of blue / Beckon silent in the night. / Organ sighs, inferno laughs, / And a horror grips the heart . . . —Sister, when I found you by a lonely glade / In the woods, at noon, and the animal's silence was vast . . . — . . .The sister's pale form stepped from putrefying blue and thus spake her bleeding mouth: Prick black thorn . . .* —Didn't such lines, to cap it all, point blatantly to incest?—Was it really true, as I'd once heard, that Trakl had defiled his own sister?

What was this morass in which I'd lost my way?

Where was it—the thought flashed through my mind—wherever was it that Marx spoke of Egypt, where brothers slept with their sisters, and that that had been respectable, because it was the norm?—I flipped through what books I had of Marx, already realizing how pointless it was to search for this passage; after all, we weren't living in the Pharaonic Age.—Was there any point in weighing things against each other; what was I trying to prove with these quotes?—*Prick black thorn.*

Aimlessly I leafed through Trakl's poems: *The spirit of evil gazes from pale masks*—oh, it grinned from all these poems, or no, it had no need to grin, it gazed calmly, fate, cold splendour of infernal light.—Hell rose up from these lines, but the most horrible thing was that these verses still appealed to me, no, 'appealed' was the wrong word: that these verses still agitated me, that these verses still beguiled me, that these verses still drove me mad—what was going on?—I knew what it was, yet I failed to grasp it.—I was already incapable, all too often, of sober thought; I'd grown addicted to alcohol, something to numb the daily contradictions that ground away at me—did this go hand in hand with addiction to the numbing verses of the decadents?—But alcohol revolted me, I abhorred it and drank it all the same, I saw it as an odious enemy I grappled and grappled with, only to succumb, over and over, disgusting myself—that wasn't what my relationship to Trakl was like! Alcohol clouded my gaze and drew a veil over daily life; but Trakl had opened my eyes to see night's riddled brow and the blind clock-hands climbing towards midnight; he had lit up my consciousness, though with the fiery glow of Hell; his verses had shaken my mad delusion that German arms would claim the final victory; and now I was asked to curse him as my enemy, like the swill I drank to flee from thought?—I could not, for he was my brother; then again, it dismayed me that he remained so: it was only logical to see him as an enemy! *Tertium non datur*—there

was no third way!—Or was there?—But no, I reached
for the bottle to numb this question as well and felt the
admonishing gaze of my teacher, who had given us new
faith, new hope, new assurance, new consciousness. He
too had had a harrowing struggle to free himself from
the bonds of the old, the dear, familiar things that
throughout his childhood and youth had penetrated and
pervaded all the fibres of his being. From a family of
pastors, he had cleansed himself to become an atheist; he
set an example that it was possible to transform oneself
rigorously, that is, in exactly the places where the
ruptures were most painful. He had let us gaze into his
breast, the battlefield between reaction and progress, and
now I saw him standing before me once more, eying me
calmly, sadly, personally wounded: had he taught me
nothing whatsoever?

Coming after the trivial pedantry of my school days,
what had fascinated me about Marxist literary history—
Lenin's essays on Leo Tolstoy or Georg Lukács' disquisi-
tions on progress and reaction in German literature
—was the greater sociohistorical context within which
writers' works began to reveal their essence in a way I'd
never known before. Now this context linked decadence
and fascism—why did I make an exception for Trakl? I
drew the logical conclusion mentally but not emotionally:
new mentality and old emotions; what a mishmash I
was! And yet the conclusion was irrefutable: what took
place in Trakl's poems was a dismantling of the 'humanly

good'—words of Hölderlin's that had filled me with bliss, feeling that they anticipated all the nobility, truth, goodness and beauty that socialism would set free—wasn't that true? I had to admit that it was, which led to the next question: Didn't this dismantling of the humanly good serve the agenda of humanity's enemies, the escalation of the Cold War into a hot war, already raging in Korea?—It all made sense; why did I resist?—Vestiges of the old.—I travelled to West Berlin to stuff strangers' mailboxes with flyers condemning the impending war—shouldn't I have begun by addressing one to myself? Didn't I grasp the dictate of the moment, and if I thought I grasped it, why did I draw my conclusions only half-heartedly, confining them to the politics of the day and leaving out other spheres, as though some precinct could exist aloof from world events?

In this very precinct one was constantly exhorted to increase one's vigilance. At a consultation with artists and writers in March 1951, my society's authority on cultural questions sternly rebuked the novelist Arnold Zweig; Zweig had spoken out against the condemnation of Paul Dessau's Lucullus opera (supposedly too formalistic and thus unfit to mobilize the masses in the struggle for peace) by arguing that in ten years today's listeners would get used to Dessau's music, just as shocked Rococo audiences had warmed to the avant-garde sounds of a certain Mozart: 'Dear Comrade Zweig'—said the ideologue to the writer—'The threat of war will not wait ten years and I must stress once again that the struggle for progressive art is part of our great struggle for peace!'—And the writer had found no response.— This music, of all things, had appealed to me as well, even after that condemnation, just as Trakl's poems still transported me—things couldn't go on like this! I was still mired so deeply in the Old! True, I was putting my life on trial and my verdict of guilt was honest, but this reckoning took place in my consciousness; what was playing out beneath it? *A pale angel / The son steps inside his father's empty house*—which house was my home? This tenement on Berlin's Linienstrasse, this wretched furnished room where not even a footstool belonged to me, the walls a jumble of junk souvenirs, spectres of the bourgeois philistines I hated, and in my dreams I sat in the leather armchair and my father scribbled his formulae —the poison in the fox's mouth, the herb of sweet dreams, O our lost paradise.—Did my homeland lie in the past after all?—In my dreams it rose before me.—I raged against these dreams; my homeland was the new society. *There is a room, and they've whitewashed it with milk*—what stared out beneath the whitewash, what was the dead man writing on the wall in the basement vaults?—A grinning silence; face eaten away.—Where did flesh melt away to; where did consciousness go?

O *you psalms in the fiery rain of midnight*; then, re-reading this 'Psalm': *The strange sister reappears in some-one's evil dreams resting in the hazels she is playing with*

his stars the student perhaps a doppelganger gazes after
her from the window his dead brother stands behind him
or walks down the old spiral stairs—I understood not a
word, yet these words spoke my fate, behind me stood
my dead brother, the doppelgänger *I*, did Trakl have
brothers, I had none, was I split in two, I didn't know.—
I didn't want to be reading this, why was I reading this,
and I watched myself reading it though I didn't want to
be reading and watching, and watched myself watching,
and watched this too and spun in a maelstrom and
beheld myself, that sinking Other, and in this Other's evil
dreams the strange sister reappeared, the wife of a colleague who had been arrested by our security forces in
the middle of the night at a conference in Weimar, evidently on the basis of some slander; I hadn't met her
before, but I knew who she was the moment she walked
in and asked about the man who had vanished without
a trace. We were duty bound to know nothing; I saw her
face, riven by anxiety, compose itself in mute contempt;
she saw through our baseness; and she went out; and I
did not follow her.—'Let others speak of their shame; I
speak of my own.'—Back then I too recited these words
by Brecht; they were an admonition about my past, and
as I remembered it, I pulled myself together. What was I
thinking: the past was still alive, our security forces
surely knew what they had to do to fight a foe who
threatened the life of our young state, this true fatherland
of the people which Goethe had glimpsed and Hölderlin

had yearned for: free soil for a free people, united in the bliss of peaceful labour, protected by the guard with the flaming sword, yes indeed, the guard who was cruel today to reign kindly tomorrow. And though till then Hölderlin's angel had been nothing but a fine-sounding word, now I saw him shine out incarnate as once the angel of the fatherland did, prodigious, bristling with snow-white brilliance; and then, outside on the rubble, I saw the brother of the radiant one huddling before him, wings wrapped around his body as though chilled by the gleaming angel's snow, and his wings were faeces-stained and he looked at me with mournful eyes and worms dripped from his lids, or he went down the stairs where a strange sister had descended, still hanging outside askew in the air, over the roaming dogs and the scenes of the fires, and for one heartbeat I recognized the angel of my fatherland, a fatherland that was the Other to Auschwitz all the same.—Faeces-stained, what an outrage! And at that my *I* was no longer split; it was an ordinary day, with the sort of ordinary decision that thousands of people have to make; I snatched the book, just as, filled with loathing, I sometimes snatched a full bottle to hurl it into the refuse pit and out of my existence —I snatched the book to tear it up and burn the scraps, and could I have mustered the strength to do it, my path would have been a different one.—Poetry works like fate: the black cardboard merely tore and the match went unused.

Later, after an attack of clear-eyed despair, I confessed to a superior that failed attempt at self-mastery; he stared at me dumbfounded and said, shaking his head: Well, if you really take those things so seriously . . . ! —and then he spoke of other things. His remark was a counsel, showing great trust and unusual openness; he wanted to save me from a calamity, but it was no longer in his power.

4.

Décadence. The *Dictionary of Cultural Policy* (2nd EDN, 1978) defines this phenomenon and concept as follows:

Decadence: philosophical-aesthetic term for the decay and deformation of the relations, morals and norms of human coexistence, for the gradual surrender of humanist principles of social organization. Since the late nineteenth century, *decadence* has also been used as a term for the artistic reflection of these social phenomena. With the transition to imperialism, and its aesthetic expression in works of art and literature, *decadence* has necessarily established itself as a widespread tendency in the intellectual life of the ruling imperialistic bourgeois class. For the most part it serves an apologist function. In literature and art, *decadence* manifests itself primarily by altering the realistic image of humanity and secondarily, as a consequence of this deformation of the object, by certain aesthetic choices. These crucial alterations to typical modes of human behaviour within a given social reality and the artistic generalization of these alterations are based on objective social processes. As a consequence of man's exploitation by man, alienation emerges as the defining characteristic of all interpersonal relations within the antagonistic class society, above all within imperialism. Alienation leads to the dehuman-ization of interpersonal relations. The process of alienation is reflected in ideological and philosophical tendencies and through them influences artists' aesthetic assessment of man and man's fundamental situation. In turn, the ruling ideology integrates this objective phenomenon in an apologist spirit, interpreting this aesthetic evaluation as the only possible position to be taken towards serious art and literature. In this way, critical components of the aesthetic view of mankind are converted into impotent resignation. Since the emergence of socialism—the actual social alternative—the ruling ideology of imperialism has become less and less successful in committing the majority of artists to this aesthetic concept.

Well, let us stop here. The article traces, in its fashion, the fate of decadence and its exponents beyond Trakl's time to our day, and raises several questions to which we have no real answers but which we hope will offer us a new perspective on Trakl's poetry.

If decadence is defined as the 'the decay and deformation of the relations, morals and norms of human coexistence, . . . the gradual surrender of humanist principles of social organization' and the 'dehumanization of interpersonal relations', and decadence in literature and art is viewed as the reflection (rendition, portrayal, expression, translation, etc.) of this surrender of humanity, this presupposes that human relations in that social structure were harmonious before falling into decay. Accordingly, society in the industrial age, from the late absolutism of the Holy Alliance to the Bismarck era of 'Blood and Iron' and including the Biedermeier, Wilhelmine and Victorian periods, must have been a world of humane relationships that decayed—was that so?—Certainly, all interpersonal relations, even in wolfish epochs, contain to a greater or lesser degree elements that anyone with a positive view of the term 'humanist' could construe as 'humane' (to take an extreme example: in the relations between the condemned and the hangman, the principle of swift execution might make death by hanging, by the axe, even by fire, more merciful than that from bladder cancer or from asthma)—every interpersonal relationship, every norm of human coexistence, every social infrastructure is a contradictory unity of humane and inhumane. But in the decay of a society, would only the humane decay and only the inhumane take its place?—That is hard to accept—it would amount to a worldview of radical historical pessimism, standing in strange contradiction to official optimism.

Or, as this definition of decadence alludes less to some law of history than to a concrete society, would that society (disregarding private ownership of the major means of production) thus be the humane society per se, as dictated by natural law, quite in keeping with ultra-bourgeois rhetoric? Oh, that highly instructive longing for the Good Old Days—how else to interpret regrets over the decay of the world of Louis Bonaparte and Kaiser Wilhelm, of Franz Joseph, Tsar Nikolai and the Queen? Or what are they lamenting then, these campaigners against decadence who see themselves as revolutionaries? Is it their own springtime, the historic time of their hope? Or is it the decay of time-tested power that pains them, the once-so-solid system of order, regimen, cleanliness, discipline and obedience?—It would be good if they could specify *whose* decay so saddens them that they decry a global movement whose literature, after all, includes Baudelaire, Rimbaud, Verlaine, Mallarmé, Flaubert, Proust, Poe, Swinburne, Wilde, Ady, Krúdy, Blok, Chekhov, Schnitzler, Rilke, Hofmannsthal, Trakl and Halas, to name just a few, and *The White House* and *The Blue Bird* and *Buddenbrooks* and *The Goddesses, or The Three Novels of the Duchess of Assy.*—Need not a historical definition differentiate just *what* was decayed and *what* was humane about it, and if one criticizes decadence for failing to show a way out and a goal to aim for, shouldn't one investigate, if not appreciate, what it brought into awareness when it showed that what seemed solid was in fact decaying?—Cracks in the walls;

what is revealed behind them?—Surely humanity as well; might it not be released by this decay like the prisoner by the earthquake in Chile? And if decay calls a social order into question, doesn't it also ask what its Other might be, even if it cannot yet articulate it?—Its Other, not its derivation: the way out of a building belongs to the building; if it collapses, the way out is usually buried as well—shouldn't it be possible to ask what the collapse might lay open? *There—decay breathes soft and makes me shudder*—at what? *When peace tolls with the church bells in the evening, / I trace the birds' miraculous migrations, / Long gatherings like pious pilgrimages / Which vanish into autumn's clear expanses. // A-wander in the garden's waning light / I daydream of their brighter destinies / And scarcely feel the hour-hand advance. / Thus over the clouds I trace their journeys.*

There—decay breathes soft and makes me shudder— what is decaying in this Trakl poem that has 'Decay' as its title? The poem does not tell us; it only shows the symptoms: *The blackbird laments amid the barren branches. / At rusty gratings scarlet vine-leaves tremble. // And like a dance of death by pale children / Around the rims of fountains dark and weathering / Blue asters bow down shivering in the wind.*—What is decaying?—The peace of the garden, but what is its peace?—An idyll, but wherein is it idyllic?—In illusory appearance.—For the lovely garden has decayed: barren branches, lamenting blackbirds, rusty gratings, pale children, dances of death, weathering fountains, dark paths, shivering asters, the peaceful world is lost, only you haven't noticed yet, dreamily you've followed the birds' miraculous flights, the magic of their signs upon the clear sky making you forget that they're leaving the land where this garden lies: *Over the white pond / The wild birds have taken flight. / In the evening an icy wind blows from our stars.*—For the moment the asters shiver while the dreamer is at ease.—After autumn comes winter; is that what the poem is saying?—This irrefutable truth hardly calls for Trakl's verses; they awaken us to a different thing, the sweetness of this decay; the reader shivers, and, we admit, so do we.—A dance of death by pale children, and the blue flower dies of cold.—Can we escape all these frightening questions by seizing on an antinomy, when the poem speaks of *autumn's clear expanses* in which the birds vanish but also of the clouds over which they fly?— Ah, but this is no contradiction: one thing is the landscape before your eyes and the other is the land that your gaze cannot reach.—Or shall we flee to Schiller's treatise on the reason for our enjoyment of tragic subjects, adding to them the subjects of pity?—Schiller is always worth studying; we commend him to the reader, but we are not entirely prepared to accept his comforting notion that the 'dance of death' is a mere image in the realm of aesthetic semblance; this 'mere' is an insult to poetry, and our affect, not springing from theory, cannot be overcome through speculation.

A dance of death by pale children: what makes Trakl's poem so sweet?

His sound, certainly; but it isn't music.—This seems an opportune moment to express our view that the freightedness of a word with the plural *Worte* includes its freightedness with the tonal associations offered by the language: the word *Mond*, for example, is linked with the words *Mohn* and *Mund* and *Mord*,[17] in a way that links their poetic notions as well, and a crucial aspect of modern poetry is that it consciously reveals this freightedness or, better, that it taps it as a poetic element.—Yet the sound does not exhaust the sense; all attempts at such reductionism have failed instructively.—What makes up the sweetness, then? This exquisite peace, certainly; but also its destruction?—Also its destruction, precisely its destruction; destruction is of the essence of this sonnet, maintaining the element of aesthetic uniformity: lovely, tranquilly drifting images, vivid and clearly defined with a lovely, darkly tranquil tone. The images of a surrender to dreaming precisely mirror those of the rude awakening, and the *dance of death* and the *pilgrimages* relate to each other in a special way: they are metaphoric elements that point into the social reality rather than away from it. In the Alpine lands near Italy, pilgrims to Rome are at least periodically part of the daily life to which the consumptive factory workers' children belong entirely while in the lovely garden they don't belong at all: only Trakl's sonnet puts them there, and nothing could have forced it to do so. The poem does not compare emaciated children with flowers; it compares flowers with emaciated children, and this reversal creates the emphasis. If the metaphor went in the other direction—mind you, the question we are about to ask, even if answered in the affirmative, would not negate *what else* (not only in the art of decadence) this metaphor undertakes to do—if the metaphor went in the other direction, it would be difficult not to ask whether the poem is attempting to distil a poetic charm from social hardship and human suffering. But here the question breaks down: the poetic charm of Trakl's sonnet affects us on account of this human suffering; rather than idealizing pain, his metaphor lucidly reveals it, though we must first take the thorny path of these questions. —The shock of this image in this language makes us wince; were it a wince of embarrassment, we would be untouched.—Is this social criticism, then?

Sigh—

Let us walk once more through this decay.

When peace tolls with the church bells in the evening, / I trace the birds' miraculous migrations, / Long gatherings like pious pilgrimages / Which vanish into autumn's clear expanses.—This stanza surely needs no explaining; still, let us point out how much meaning it gains if *long* is seen not only, and not so much, as a spatial description of the airborne procession but also as a hint that the pilgrimage has been long in the gathering.— Decay is not a sudden cave-in, many things lead up to it, and the birds' departure is the result of many subtle changes, not of an abrupt resolution. But that is something readers already knew. *A-wander in the garden's waning light / I daydream of their brighter destinies*; do readers feel in *destinies* something a shade of meaning away from 'fate', something that is not merely a blindly working doom, but the capacity for determination, and also—here, too, more than in 'fate'—the echo of 'destined' as well as 'destination', both accenting the subject's active role?—Seed of a question: What condemns the dreamer to linger in the garden's waning light? Is there someone who could send him, too, to the destination where brighter things unfold?—Ah, the poem too is such a garden (*This passing strange garden / Of darkling trees / Filled with serpents, hawk-moths, / Spiders and bats*).—*There is a vineyard, burnt and black with holes full of spiders*—There is your land, and you abide. —The destinies of those in flight are brighter: O our lost paradise!

I daydream of their brighter destinies / And scarcely feel the hour-hand advance. / Thus over the clouds I trace their journeys. // There—decay breathes soft and makes me shudder—This poem's prodigious word is *there*: it concentrates time and place, voicing the concreteness of an abstraction.—Trakl was suffering through an era of disintegrating value systems and lives governed by anonymous powers; emotions that once had concrete reference points were transformed into abstract emotions lacking reference. When you can no longer make out whom to fear, the fear of specific things becomes fear as such; an aversion to this or that becomes loathing of everything; the sight of a concrete ruin turns to the dull sense of general decay, and sorrow over a distinct loss becomes a universal surge of lamentation.—It is the evening twilight or the late autumn that best expresses this indistinctness. *My dear Sir! Enclosed please find the two signed contracts. If you would like the collection to be given a different title, I suggest the one it originally had,* Twilight and Decay. *I believe it expresses all that is essential,* Trakl wrote to his publisher Kurt Wolff. In previous generations this indistinctness coalesced into the sated world-weariness best described with Flaubert's word 'ennui', or Baudelaire's 'spleen', into that totality of complexly intangible unease some of whose nuances (but never the whole) are reflected in translations such as 'boredom', 'melancholy', 'disgust with life', 'languor', 'inadequacy'. But Trakl and his kindred spirits no longer succumbed to this ennui, only the epigones still indulged in it. Ennui is tied to security; it is a weariness with the existing world which one knows to be solid: 'I'm like some king in whose corrupted veins / Flows agèd blood; who rules a land of rains; / Who, young in years, is old in all distress; / Who flees good counsel to find weariness / Among his dogs and playthings, who is stirred / Neither by hunting-hound nor hunting-bird; / Whose weary face emotion moves no more / E'en when his people die before his door',[18] as Baudelaire writes in the third of his four great poems of spleen in *Les Fleurs du Mal.* This world still seems unassailably powerful; Trakl's poem already speaks of its decay, not only the poem called 'Decay' but his entire *oeuvre*, which is itself one great poem, and it speaks of decay in all its aspects, from horror at seeing the solid ground gape at your feet to the sweetness of final repose: decay, too, as a longing for decay, as a falling for the fall into decay, as an intense satisfaction in ruin.—The double meaning of *midnight*.—This totality of the process of decay that takes form in Trakl's poem-as-a-whole allows us, against all philological rules, to move from one poem to another, from the garden of 'Decay' to the garden called 'Sleep', and soon back into the garden of the 'Psalm' where it is evening, where bats flutter in its cloisters, where the dead orphans seen before in their dance now lie by the wall.— Readers should not be shy of moving freely in Trakl's world, the world of his ever-recurring words and images; only thus will they gain access to what lies before their eyes. These words and images have been catalogued and counted;[19] here we might note that the word and image of the evening appears in nearly three quarters of all his poems, autumn in almost half of them and the word 'garden' in one quarter.—But back to our poem.

There—*decay breathes soft and makes me shudder*— a breath, no more, prevailing over the chiming bells, and 'shudder' is the most intense of all verbs that could be used here; it implies the strongest physicality. It is the word Schiller used to exact the most menacing possible effect: 'Before the slave who breaks his chains, / Before the free man do not shudder!'—*There*—and a breath and a shudder; *The blackbird laments amid the barren branches*—its song transformed by the breath of decay, no longer a synonym for 'melodious' and 'sweet'.— Sometimes in Trakl it sounds that way still, on that *Evening, when on the twilight wall the blackbird sang,* a *Dark breath in green branches.*—In Trakl the cheerful cuckoo laments too: *In the evening the lament of the cuckoo / Fades in the woods;* and these sounds are heard even on high: *Sadness! lament of lonely eagles.*—That is the last line of a poem itself called 'Lament', and two others are called the same.

At rusty gratings scarlet vine-leaves tremble—who disturbs it? Is the wind blowing?—That was only a breath just now. The image is more than naturalistic; nature partakes in the physical tumult.—Yet some other thing makes the scarlet vine-leaves tremble, just as some other thing makes its beholder shudder; everything here is both outward and inward, and outside because it's in and inside because it's out.—A mere breath, and red— freightedness of the *Wort* with the plural *Worte*—segues into *rusty*.

There—decay breathes soft and makes me shudder. / The blackbird laments amid the barren branches. / At rusty gratings scarlet vine-leaves tremble. // And like a dance of death by pale children / Around the rims of fountains dark and weathering / Blue asters bow down shivering in the wind. Not 'around weathered fountain rims', but around *the rims of fountains dark and weathering*; the verb is active, the decay is advancing, though you see only the result, not the process. And only in the last line does the wind spring up, a strange wind. Its coolness may materialize that breath of decay that made the dreamer shudder; still, that in its passing asters bow down *around* the rims of fountains is difficult to picture. That is not how wind blows, and besides, there are several fountains: they are in the plural—in *one* garden? Like the procession of birds, the sonnet points past its walls: it is the land and the era that are decaying and around its fountains, dark and weathering, is the pale children's dance of death.

Let us at last face the question inevitably raised by this sort of analysis: whether we aren't creating a mystique around the details, which might have sprung from formal considerations such as rhyme constraints or the demands of rhythm. It is in the nature of great poetry, we reply, that it *can* be analysed this way, that its details always fit, in short, that its creator manipulates the forms, not the forms his poem. Otherwise it would be like explaining the logic of a masterfully played chess game not by the player's mastery but by claiming that the pieces, with the specific moves they can make, were always set up in his favour—yet moved by a master's hand, they are always set up favourably, arrayed in a way that favours his game. That this unfolding and

self-unfolding of the poem always far transcends its creator's intent, that structures, relationships, references,
consequences emerge objectively from subjectively chosen poetic elements, is another matter entirely.

A *dance of death by pale children*—this image
demands to be confronted. Its beauty causes that pain
that both fends off and forces further thought. This
dance of death is no longer the medieval dance of death
where young lives, blanching, fall in line. 'Alas, fair maid,
your cheeks' bright flower / Shall pale here within the
hour': in that circle dance in the cemetery of Basel's
Dominican Monastery all society shows itself arm in arm
with skeletons, a powerful memento mori and yet a
triumph of life, which in the self-awareness of social
endurance dares to depict itself alongside that force in
whose embrace a human being is nothing but human—
mortals all, from the emperor down to the beggar, but
each representing his class and the long duration of this
class: *The king is dead, long live the king*! Here, in these
dances of death, the durability of transience encompasses
endurance amid perpetual evanescence, and far more
than the notion of the soul's immortality (lesson of the
memento mori), it is society's perseverance that comes to
the fore: solid, earthly, certain in its duration. No decay
breathes soft and makes one shudder, though what is
invoked is the moment at which the flesh starts falling
from the bones.—The refusal to suppress death shows
these mortals' existential certainty; their 'in the midst of

life we are in death' is truly a thought from life's midst,[20] and to see the final hour as a dance is to behold death from amid the fullness of life, not life from the void of deadness (for 'Death' personified is no void). In the dances of death, 'Death' acts in the flesh; at the same time each dancer is 'Life' and each life has its own death.—In the modern poem death vanishes as a personage; its passage into abstraction was conjured by Rilke with surrealistic concreteness: 'There stands death, a bluish extract / in a cup without a saucer.'[21]

In Auschwitz, it was a bluish haze.

A dance of death by pale children—the skeletal dancer is missing here, the society whose decay racks the garden is invisible, and the members of society who reel out to die are those most intimately bound with our notion of life.—This dance too springs from Trakl's daily life: consumption was a social problem, tuberculosis an unchecked epidemic on a scale barely imaginable today. The pain of the young Edvard Munch—to take just one example—as his sister Sophie waned away in torment made him create ten renditions of the subject that thrust him onto his artistic trajectory:

> In the sick child I paved new roads for myself—
> it was a breakthrough in my art.—Most of what
> I have done since had its genesis in this picture.
> No painting in Norway has elicited such a scandal.—When I entered the hall where it hung on
> opening day, people stood crowded together in

front of the picture;—shouts and laughter could be heard.[22]

A dance of death by pale children—pain chafes against outrage: a lovely image, a calmly flowing rhythm and extreme suffering described as helplessly as though the poet were revelling in it; is a poem allowed to do this? And 'pale' is a *Wort* with the plural *Worte*, not restricted to consumption; it bespeaks pallor from fear, from yearning, from grief, from a secret wound to the heart, and the thin skin of defencelessness resonates as well: this pale children's dance is not the inevitable hour which in the Gothic dance of death must come one day to all; here it stands for the dying of those needlessly carried off too soon, and the poet stands by watching—is that allowed?

This is the eternal question of the poem's capacities and thus of its purpose, and as long as poetry concerns people, the answer will be ambivalent. With radical honesty Gottfried Benn (in a fictitious dialogue, 'Can Poets Change the World?') posed and confronted the question in connection with this subject, for consumption was part of daily life then:

> I will show you a different procession. Thirty-six thousand people with open tuberculosis living in Berlin who can't get into a sanatorium; forty thousand women who die every year in Germany of the consequences of illegal abortions [. . .] Consider the following document: A family of

eleven; the father drinks; the mother is expecting her tenth child; the fourteen-year-old daughter buys cow's blood at the butcher's for ten pfennige and pours it over her breast hoping that this simulated haemorrhage will help get her out of her overcrowded apartment and into a TB sanatorium. This is misery, these are tears, innocent suffering, bastardizations of happiness—and the poet just watches?[23]

That is the self-posed question, and Benn answered it with provocative plainness and a shocking lack of equivocation, distinguishing most harshly, most rigorously, between aesthetics and ethics: 'Yes, the poet watches!'—This statement is not made in Trakl's name; our intent is not to delve into the problem but merely to ask readers who are outraged by this answer and demand that the poet do more than just watch: With their demand, don't they unconsciously pass on to some other authority an obligation which they themselves ought to fulfil where they could meaningfully do so—in the sphere of *their* everyday activity? The poet's outrage would then compensate for their failure to do their part, and with good conscience they would read of what they failed to do as of something already done.—For example, one celebrates Heine's fight against the intolerance and censorship of Metternich's bureaucracy in order to feel exempted from taking a stand against intolerance and censorship in one's own age.—Likewise with demands on poets to make us happy and confident in the future:

all too often these demands are made by the very people who do so little for these values even when it is in their power.

But that is one aspect among many; another was expressed by T. S. Eliot: 'Poetry is not a turning loose of emotion, but an escape from emotion . . . '[24]

A dance of death by pale children—reading this, we gazed deep into our life and from it rose that circle dance that affected us and none other: a soldier who resembled us, and Greek children, and Ukrainian children, and Serbian children, and children on the gallows, and children in the ice, and children in fires, and the Polish boy who ran alongside a train filled with men on leave, crying for bread as he ran until he fell, and we tossed him a piece of bread as you'd toss a dog a bone, and felt no breath of decay; there the dance abruptly broke off—yet was it really over today? Certainly, in our daily lives no one starved to death and consumption was vanquished, but what about the children of my arrested colleague— didn't they need, if not a piece of bread, at least comfort, a consoling word, a glance? And didn't the children in Trakl's poem stand for all those who pale daily in their helplessness, trembling defenceless in the cold, or in the breath of horror as *red* shades into *rusty*?

Questions that were felt—not posed—for nearly two decades, and when posed, were passed over in silence; yet realizing how the dance of death breaks off in the present, we suddenly saw too that Trakl does not compare dying children with flowers but flowers with dying children—*he* has taken the defenceless ones into his lovely garden; nothing could have forced him to do so, but he compels our fraternity with the compulsion inherent to poetry: that of an open wound, an unsoothable pain. It is for the sake of this dance, we intuit, that the poet does not follow the vanishing pilgrimages, instead lingering in the decaying garden, decaying himself as a witness to decay, himself having fallen for the process of falling, but his poem lasts and will affect readers as long as this circle dance still turns.—It has always been turning; will it ever end?—We do not believe it will; faces in the snow, and the fountains are weathering; we could surrender to an illusion, but that is just what the poet abjures: he surrenders to his helplessness.—The sweetness of evanescence, another kind of freedom; but in some mysterious way, might not the author's surrender provoke in the reader the turmoil that torments like desire amid pleasure, like perturbation in the peace of an idyll that includes death as a line revealing the perspective: *All roads end in black putrefaction*?—Or, put in the same but different words: all that comes to be deserves to perish wretchedly.[25]

The only question is whose perishing one laments, or, more than a lament, for whose sake one wishes to surrender to evanescence even as all that is dear fades away: the old fountains, the asters, the pale children. The fraternal solidarity that asserts itself in this evanescence by surrendering is itself a special kind of decay: the decay of fraternity with the strong, the decay of the order of the orderly, the healthy, fit, productive. Those who count themselves among this class prefer not to fraternize outside it, for then they would be no longer what they boundlessly desire to be—orderly, strong, healthy: in short, normal.—But this decay sets free something human and introduces it as a new poetic element; incidentally, never for the first time.—The decadence that called itself Christianity taught us to honour our brother and sister in those hitherto despised, and set the slave, the prisoner, the sick, the poor on equal footing with the free and the rich; that was outrageous indeed, the decay of a historic order, and Christianity was rebuked for it, most harshly by Nietzsche, the foe of all decadence, who was proud to be a decadent himself. 'The New Testament is the gospel of a wholly ignoble species of man . . .'[26]—'Christianity has absorbed diseases of all kinds from morbid soil: one can only reproach it for its inability to guard against any infection. But that precisely is its essence: Christianity is a type of decadence.'[27] It was left to other detractors of decadence to draw up literary blacklists detailing what authors must, on pain of proscription, regard as non-subjects; they list the sick and the weak, the atypical, the abnormal, the homosexuals, the psychopaths, the failures and the wrecks—oh, the longing for the Good Old Days, when it was so natural and normal to classify the psychopath as asocial, the homosexual as criminal, the Other as a foe. But has that time really fallen by the wayside? Would it not be a shocking proposal, even here and now, to see the Otherness of other sexual behaviour not as an abhorrent abnormality but as an enrichment to the human emotional experience? Or to see in the world of the neurotic not mere confusion but also insight concealed to the normal gaze? Or to take seriously this line by Trakl: *And what is golden and true is oft revealed to gentle madness.*—A breath of decay?—We take it seriously.

But before we end this train of thought with the only thing that can conclude it, Trakl's reclaimed poem, which still torments us in its sweetness as the rims of the fountains go on weathering and the children's dance goes on turning—before we end our train of thought, we remind the reader that what recurs in the poem is not only an outside but an inside, an inside that is not a mere mirror of outside events but a realm with a might of its own.— An autumn of the soul is not only the reflection of autumn as a natural phenomenon, it is also a thing of its own, but one that would never find form in words if it could not be captured in a metaphor, as in the metaphor of autumn and decay. The modernist poem from Baudelaire to József and Lautréamont to Halas has laid open precincts of this realm that one trembles to behold; but they are precincts within us, and fraternity might begin by—or lead to—considering the possibility of these precincts in the *I* in order to see part of one's self in the

Other. A *dance of death by pale children*, and helpless-ness, and sweetness, and pain, and trembling; if the reader dares to gaze into everyday life, he should also venture to gaze inside himself and realize: I am this as well. He can find guidance in the words of a founder of modernism, dead of consumption at twenty-four, Isidore-Lucien Ducasse alias Comte de Lautréamont, whose *Songs of Maldoror* are one of the most candid documents of the gaze into the soul's abyss: 'Laughter, evil, pride and madness will appear in turn along with sensibility and the love of justice, and will be an example, to the utter astonishment of all men: everyone will recognize himself in my work, not as he ought to be, but as he is.'[28]

It is not possible always, and everywhere, to gaze into one's own soul; readers must seek a favourable hour and if possible a favourable place. Such as this one: *When peace tolls with the church bells in the evening, I trace the birds' miraculous migrations, long gatherings like pious pilgrimages which vanish into autumn's clear expanses. A-wander in the garden's waning light I day-dream of their brighter destinies and scarcely feel the hour-hand advance. Thus over the clouds I trace their journeys. There—decay breathes soft and makes me shudder. The blackbird laments amid the barren branches. At rusty gratings scarlet vine-leaves tremble. And like a dance of death by pale children around the rims of fountains dark and weathering blue asters bow down shivering in the wind.*

I have spoken of my attempt to destroy Trakl's verse within me by destroying his books in my possession and was forced to confess that I failed. It is useful to think through my experience of this failure. At first it bewildered me; then it filled me with an ever-fiercer mixture of self-reproach over my lack of rigour and secret satisfaction in this force that made me shun rigour's ultimate conclusion: these bridges I sought to burn and could not—weren't they also bridges from myself to myself?—Later I shrank at Heine's words 'Where they burn books, they will end by burning people', but that, I admit, came later. At the time I deemed it dialectical to regard the burning of 'bad' books as 'good' and that of 'good books' as 'bad'; in this distinction between good and bad my society's world seemed intact and in this intactness ideal. The world within me had already ceased to be so, but to me it seemed it was *not yet* so: Distant bliss that shines up close, but working against it are the relics of the Old—how much longer? In war captivity, at the school, I'd thought that they were overcome and that I was in full accord with my new society; was the grip of the Old so tenacious and covert? I felt a sense of disquiet, as doubts, as brooding, as inadequacy, but were these phenomena really 'the Old' and was this really how the Old worked? Had my past been marked by doubts and brooding? Was this increasingly urgent question—by virtue of what existential perfection did one part of society determine for us all, definitively yet without definition, what was *white = good* and what was *black = bad*?—really only a relic of fascism; might it not be an attempt to overcome backward thought? Such questions flashed through my self-reproaches and I shuddered at the sacrilege.—O, *how ancient is our race.*—I drank; the questions faded and lingered; I watched them make their rounds, like ghosts, and drank.—I discovered the realm of intoxication in the Trakl poem: *A yellow slanted haystack flees through greyness / And sometimes you float so wondrous and light*—a 'Ramble' in an ecstasy of wine, ranging from the rare exultation of *Sublime is the taste of nuts and young wine. / Sublime: to reel drunk through the darkening woods* to the end point of 'On the Way': O, *how dark is this night. A purple flame / Went out at my lips. In the stillness / The lonely music of the anxious soul's strings fades. / Leave be, when drunk with wine the head sinks in the gutter.*—Did these lines confirm my hangover? Again I tried to hate them, but knew perfectly well what I hated was that I had fallen for alcohol, I hated alcohol and in it myself who fled these questions instead of facing their insistence rightly: with a consciousness that seeks truth. But surely the desire for clarity and truth was no relic of the Old; or did a dialectic such as J.N.Z. had propounded to us at school hold true here as well; did an excess of truth suddenly turn into—well, what? Into a lie? Into evil?

Pondering the truth— / Much pain.

Amid all this dark, tormented brooding, the lightning bolt of a party congress struck.

I am not writing an autobiography; I am telling of my experience with the poem of Georg Trakl and must refrain from describing the days of cathartic dismay brought on by the 20th Congress of the Communist Party of the Soviet Union with Nikita Khrushchev's momentous speech at the closed evening session.[29] I shall report only one personal consequence: it helped me stop drinking for more than three years.—Never had the certain hope of invincible truth shone so brightly.—In its light the Trakl poem suddenly seemed unreal; *twilight and decay*, what was that to me now that day was breaking, what were these tidings from another epoch? At the same time my attempted book-burning seemed laughable and beneath me, and I formed a different resolution. The lesson drawn from that party congress was to march on ahead, leaving the Old behind, no longer to gaze back at yesterday but to stride into the morning, unwavering in the knowledge of the change that had come to pass. Now 'the Old', the officially rejected, included traits of the new society, and Stalin was a classic no longer. Properly speaking, this 'Old' already included Khrushchev's speech.—Grasping the lesson of the onward march as an exhortation to act, not discuss, I responded with a willing 'Yes!' That was when I began to discover the great, nearly unknown poets of our eastern and south-eastern neighbours: Attila József, Vítězslav Nezval, Hristo Botev, and as my own poetic efforts, for reasons I failed to grasp, faltered and petered out entirely, I turned to translation. I had begun exploring the work of Nezval, making preliminary translation attempts, and believed I had found someone who, while equal in stature to Trakl, set up the Other to be affirmed against all that I criticized more vehemently than ever as decadent: the vital, not the morbid; reconstruction, not decay; laughter, not grief; light, not dark; optimism, not pessimism—in short, one who was to Trakl as a photograph is to its negative.

The comparison was as absurd as all black and white formulae, which after all can always be constructed somehow; this one could even be turned on its head, but all we knew then of Nezval's work was, in Kurt Bartel's ravishing translation, the 'Song of Peace', indeed a splendid example of the potential of hopeful poetry; and then there were two or three poems just as masterfully translated by Louis Fürnberg which brightened this impression still further. When I found that Nezval's great Prague poems contained litany-like passages begging to be translated with 'Es ist',[30] the conviction seized me that Nezval was the Other to Trakl and that the one could replace the other just as action in the present for the future could replace the critical gaze into the past and the gaze from the past to the present.—This was still two-dimensional thinking, in black and white terms.— The scope was now expanded and yet again restricted: the work of Georg Lukács and Ernst Bloch, living classics, were eliminated from public consciousness. But the expansion as well as the restriction (or the expansion as restriction) remained strictly linear: good legacy, bad legacy, purely ideological definitions.

So Nezval took Trakl's place, and I recall writing to my friend and mentor Ludvík Kundera to tell him of my discovery, explicitly mentioning the '*Es ist*'. Kundera, who brilliantly translated Trakl into Czech, must have shaken his head in puzzlement; if I am not mistaken, I had written that I saw the possibility of 'setting up an antithesis to the "Psalm" that has had such a disastrous influence on our literature.'

Were I a literary scholar, I ought to discuss these influences now, Trakl's indisputable influence on the Czech poem and Arthur Rimbaud's indisputable influence on both Georg Trakl and Vitězslav Nezval, that famous '*il y a*' in 'Enfance', which Rimbaud's first German translator, K. L. Ammer, translated as '*es ist*':

> *Il y une horloge qui ne sonne pas.*
> *Il y a une fondrière avec un nid de bêtes blanches*—[31]

But I claim no expert knowledge. I shall share both poems and leave it to readers to make their discoveries, as doubtless they will. Perhaps they will reflect that not only Trakl's total *oeuvre* but also modernism around the globe represents one great poem, the sum of our epoch in which humankind is compelled to constitute itself as humankind and a fraternity of poetry and art leads the way. Also in Nezval and Rimbaud, the invoking of fairy tales; in Nezval and Rimbaud, the echo of the Psalms; in Nezval and Rimbaud, childhood; in Nezval and Rimbaud, the sea and the distant island; in Nezval and

Rimbaud, the global catastrophe; in Rimbaud, the stairs, the dead, the orphan, the sister; in Nezval, the madman, a figure, I confess, that still haunts me. It haunted me while I translated Nezval, and though I attempted to lose Trakl to him, he brought me back to Trakl.—Poetry works like fate which likes to work in roundabout ways. From Nezval I came to Czech Poetism, from Poetism to the Surrealists, from the Surrealists to Baudelaire and Jarry, from both of them back to decadence and, to counteract them, back again—but not as before—to Nezval, founder of Czech Surrealism; and now I translated his 'Woman in Plural', that great hymn to Prague's whores: 'But on a moonlit night her shadow sinks into the quicklime in the court behind the brickyard',[32] and suddenly I wanted to know everything about Trakl and began to study his biography.—*Twilight and decay.*

But first, here are the brothers of the 'Psalm':

Arthur Rimbaud, 'Childhood'

I

An idol . . .
Black eyes, yellow hair;
Without parents or home,
Nobler than Flemish or Mexican fables;
His empire, in blues and insolent greens,
Spreads over beaches savagely named
In Greek, Celtic or Slavic
By the shipless waves.

At the edge of the forest, where dream flowers
    chime,
Brighten and break . . .
An orange-lipped girl, her knees crossed
In the bright flood that rolls from the fields;
Nudity covered, shadowed and clothed
By rainbows, flowers and the sea.

Ladies tilting on terraces next to the sea.
Children and giants; superb black women in the
    grey-green moss,
Standing jewels in the shiny rich soil
Of groves and thawing gardens . . .
Young mothers, older sisters, with a look of
    pilgrimages in their eyes;
Sultanas, princesses, dressed and walking like
    tyrants,
Foreign little girls, and people sweetly unhappy.
What a bore, all that talk about 'dear body' and
    'dear heart'!

II

There she is, the little girl, dead behind the rose
    trees.
The young mother, deceased, descends the steps.
Cousin's carriage squeaks on the sand.
Little brother (. . . but he's in India!) is there,

In a field of carnations, before the setting sun.
The old people, already buried, stand upright in
   a flowery wall.

A swarm of golden leaves surrounds the general's
   house;
They have gone south.
You follow the red road to come to the empty
   inn.
The château is for sale; its shutters hang loose.
The priest has probably gone away with the
   key to the church.
The keepers' lodges all about the park are
   uninhabited.
The fence of the park is so high
You can only see the rattling treetops beyond.
Besides, there is nothing to see inside.

The meadows lead off to villages empty of cocks,
Empty of anvils.
The floodgates are lifted. O crosses and windmills
   of the desert!
O islands and millstones . . .

Magic flowers hummed. The slopes cradled him.
Animals of fabulous elegance wandered about.
Clouds gathered on high seas made of an eternity
   of scalding tears.

III

In the woods there is a bird;
His singing stops you, and you blush.

There is a clock that never strikes.

There is a little swamp, with a nest of pale animals.

There is a cathedral that sinks, and a lake that
rises above it.

There is a little ribbon-covered cart, abandoned
in the hedge
Or rolling away down the path.

There is a troupe of tiny strolling players all
dressed up,
Seen on the road at the edge of the woods.

And when you are hungry or thirsty,
There is always someone to chase you away.

IV

I am a saint on a terrace praying—
Like gentle beasts who graze their way to the sea
of Palestine.

I am a scholar in a dark armchair—
Branches and the rain beat at the casement of my
library.

I am a highway walker in dwarf woods—
The rush of water in the sluices drown my steps.

My eyes are full of the sad golden wash of the
sunset.

I might be an abandoned child,
Left on a causeway running into the sea;
A little lackey on a garden walk, that bumps
against the sky.

The paths are bitter,
And broom flowers cover the hills.
The air is still . . .
How far away are the birds and the fountains!
To go on can lead only to the end of the world.

V

Well, then, rent me a tomb, whitewashed and
outlined
In cement . . .
Far, far underground.

My elbows lean on the table, the lamp glares on
newspapers
I am idiot enough to reread, on books without
interest . . .

At a great distance above my underground salon,
the houses
Entrench themselves; fogs thicken . . . mud is red
or black.

Cancerous city . . .
Night without end!

The sewers are not so high above me. On all
    sides,
The breadth of the globe.
Perhaps blue depths . . . and wells of fire.
Moons in these dimensions may meet comets;
    the sea becomes myth.

In my bitter hours, I conjure up spheres of metal
    and sapphire.
I am Master of Silence.
But why should the appearance of an aperture
Gleam white in the corner of the vault?[33]

*

Vítězslav Nezval, 'Prague in the Midday Sun'

I have not woken from a dream nor arrived by
    express train
I am spared the bother of seeing the sights like a
    tourist
For years I have not opened a book of fairy tales
I don't expect love to reveal the universe or even
    this world
I don't want to sing with the birds nor rave
    about undersea landscapes
I've no illusions about nations which rule the
    world or about foreign settlements
I don't regard the people whose language I speak
    as either better or worse

than those of other countries
I'm linked with the fate of the world's disasters
and only have a little
freedom to live or die

It is late in the morning
I am sitting under a coloured parasol—Prague
lies down there
After long rains an amethyst vapour is rising
I see her through the filigree of trees as a maniac
sees his phantasm
I see her as a great ship whose mast is the Castle
Like the enchanted cities of my visions
Like the great ship of the Golden Corsair
Like the dream of delirious architects
Like the throned residence of Magic
Like Saturn's palace with its gates flung open
to the sun
Like a volcano fortress hewn by a raving
madman
Like a guide to solitary inspiration
Like an awakened volcano
Like a bracelet dangling before mirrors

It is noon
Prague is sleeping and yet awake like a fantastic
dragon
A sacred rhinoceros whose cage is the sky
A stalactite organ playing softly

A symbol of resurrection and of treasures of
  dried-up lakes
An army in panoply saluting the emperor
An army in panoply saluting the sun
An army in panoply turned into jasper

Magic city I have been gazing too long at you
  with blind eyes
Looking for you in the distance oh today I
  know it
You are obscure as the fires deep in the rocks
  as my fantasy
Your beauty has sprung from caverns and
  subterranean agates
You are old as the prairies over which song
  spreads its wings
When your tower clocks strike you are opaque
  as an island night
Exalted as the tombs as the crowns of Ethiopian
  kings
As if from a different world a mirror of my
  imagery
Beautiful as the mystery of love and improbable
  clouds
Beautiful as the mystery of speech and primor-
  dial memory
Beautiful as an erratic block marked by the rains

Beautiful as the mystery of sleep of stars and of
    phosphorescence
Beautiful as the mystery of thunder of the magic
    lamp and of poetry[34]

We promised our readers not to withhold our view
of who *the madman* in Trakl's 'Psalm' is, and we can only
say: the madman in Trakl's 'Psalm' is *the madman* in
Trakl's 'Psalm'. We have tried to show that there is no
precise answer to the question of whom Trakl might have
meant and that even if there were, this answer would rep-
resent only one—albeit extremely important—interpretation of a multifariously interpretable poem; elevating
it to the sole true interpretation would mean transforming a *Wort* with the plural *Worte* (the word 'the
madman') into a *Wort* with the plural *Wörter* (the name
of a specific madman) and thus dismantling the poem
into heterogeneity.—One who sees poems solely as products misses their seminal quality and scorns an answer
as trifling even when it holds more than he wished for.
For while each word in a poem contributes the full
freight it is laden with, the poem in turn bestows on
it its own cargo: the poem enters wholly into the word
that has offered itself wholly to the poem. In Joseph
Eichendorff's poetry the word 'forest' has drawn in every
enchantment and frisson from the spruce thickets of the
Giant Mountains to the fairy-haunted woods of folktale,
but from now on every forest shall also be his forest
'raised up there on high'.[35]—And wherever the word

'madman' appears as a *Wort* with the plural *Worte*, it is not merely all the eyes of the isolation cells that glower through its vowels, nor merely E. T. A. Hoffmann's Medardus and Shakespeare's Edgar who howl out from the bars of its consonants—after Trakl's 'Psalm', this word also houses that uninterpretable figure whose death stands between the room whitewashed with milk and an island in the South Seas.

Yet the reader was expecting something else, namely, an experience of our own with this passage as one possible interpretation, and there is indeed an association we wish to share.

The second stanza of Trakl's 'Psalm' contains the curious line *The son of Pan appears in the shape of a ditch-digger*. What son of Pan is referred to here?

Pan, according to a hymn falsely attributed to Homer, is 'the goat-footed, the twy-horned, the lover of the din of revel,'[36] son of Hermes and a daughter of the Arcadian king Dryops. He is the ancient god of shepherds, lord of the craggy mountains with their wild goat flocks; lover of all she-goats and nymphs, of midday naps and night-time dancing; creator of the pan flute and capable of the sweetest song, but also of nerve-racking shrieks and laughter (called a 'terrible scourge' by the writer of the tragedy *Rhesos*) that struck the hearer with that shock of madness that lives on in our speech as 'panic fear'.—This Pan, elemental fertility god of a mountain people far from cities, was a male of such

strong urges that it was impossible to relate all his countless daily conquests; we know only of his rejection by the
nymph Syrinx who escaped him by transforming herself
into a reed, and his love for the mountain nymph Echo,
from which sprang a daughter, Iynx, whom Hera later
transformed into a bird, the wryneck. According to
ancient tradition, Iynx is Pan's only descendent known
by name and she is unmistakeably female; there is no
word of a son, who to our knowledge first appears in
Arthur Rimbaud's prose poem 'Antique': '*Gracieux fils
de Pan*!'—'Graceful son of Pan!'

But before we turn to this son of Pan, it is essential
to note that Pan is the only Greek deity who, according
to legend, died within human history. Plutarch passed on
the account and Heinrich Heine included it in his book
on Ludwig Börne, in Book 2, between the words 'I am
tired and thirst for quiet'[37] and 'I am the son of the revolution and reach again for the invulnerable weapons':[38]

> At the time of Tiberius a ship passed one evening
> close to the Parae Islands, which lie near the
> coast of Aetolia. The people on board had not
> yet gone to sleep and many of them were sitting
> and drinking after dinner, when suddenly they
> heard a voice from the coast that cried out the
> name of Thamus (for so the helmsman was
> called) so loudly that all were highly amazed. At
> the first and second call Thamus remained silent;
> he answered the third, whereupon the voice in

amplified tones said these words to him: 'When you come up as far as Palodes, announce that great Pan has died!' When he came that far, Thamus fulfilled the instruction and cried from aft in the ship to the land: 'Great Pan is dead!' Upon this cry there followed the strangest laments, a mixture of sighing and shouting of amazement, and as though raised by many at once. The eyewitnesses told of this event in Rome, where the most peculiar opinions were expressed about it. Tiberius had the matter more closely investigated and did not doubt the truth of it.[39]

So much for Heine; now on to Rimbaud whose work—to cite Reinhold Grimm—Trakl 'did not hesitate to use as a quarry'. We happily concur with this formulation, a felicitous image for the appropriative aspect of Trakl's creativity as well as the creative character of his appropriation; the word for 'create', '*schöpfen*', also means 'to draw from what is present'. In this spirit the Romanesque and Gothic cathedrals were built from the quarries of ancient architecture, and in this spirit Trakl drew from Rimbaud, whom he first encountered in K. L. Ammer's classic translation from 1907 and later probably read in the original. In one of Rimbaud's earliest poems, '*Soleil et Chair*'—'Sun and Flesh'[40]—we now find Pan, and as in Heine, he is dead or lost:

Arthur Rimbaud, 'Sun and Flesh'

I

The sun, hearth of tenderness and life,
Spills molten love onto a grateful earth,
And, when you're asleep in a valley, you can feel
The earth beneath you, nubile and ripe with
    blood;
Her huge breast, rising with the soul within,
Is, like god, made of love; like woman, made of
    flesh;
Heavy with sap and sunlight,
And embryonic swarms.

How it all grows, how it all rises!

          —O Venus, O Goddess!
I long for the lost days of youth,
For wanton satyrs and beastly fauns,
Gods who, for love, bit the bark of branches
And kissed blonde Nymphs in water-lily pools!
I long for lost days: when the rosy blood
Of green trees, the water in rivers,
When the world's sap flowed,
Pouring a universe into Pan's veins!
When the green ground breathed beneath his
    goat's feet;
When his lips, softly kissing his syrinx,
Sent a song of love into the sky;

When, standing on the plain, he heard
Nature respond to his call;
When the silent trees cradled the songbird,
When the earth cradled man, the blue seas
And the beloved beasts—beloved in God!
I long for lost days when great Cybele
In all her boundless beauty was said
To cut across magnificent cities
In a great bronze chariot, both of her breasts
Spilling the pure stream of eternal life
Unto the breach. Mankind suckled
Her blessed breast like a delighted little child.
—Because he was strong, Man was gentle and
    chaste.

Misery! For now he says: I know everything,
And therefore wanders, eyes closed, ears shut.—
    And yet,
No more gods! No more gods! Man is King!
Man is God! But Love remains our Faith!
O Cybele! O grandmother of gods and men,
If only man could linger at your breast,
If only he hadn't forsaken immortal Astarte
Who, flower of flesh, odour of oceans,
Once rose from the vast brightness of the blue
    waves,
Baring a rosy belly snowing foam, goddess
With great black conquering eyes

Who made the nightingale sing in forests
And love in human hearts.

II

I believe in you! I believe in you! Divine mother,
Aphrodite of the sea! Oh the way is bitter
Now that another God has yoked us to his cross;
Flesh, Marble, Flower, Venus: I believe in you!
—Man is sad and ugly, sad beneath an enormous
    sky,
He is clothed for he is no longer chaste,
He has sullied his godly head,
And his Olympian body is stooped
In dirty servitude, an idol in the fire!
Yes, even in death, even as a pale skeleton
He would live on, an insult to his original
    beauty!
—And the Idol upon whom you lavished your
    virginity,
In whom you made mere clay divine, Woman,
So that Man might illuminate his poor soul
And slowly climb, in limitless love,
From the earthy prison to the beauty of light—
Woman has forgotten her virtue.
—Such a farce! And now the world snickers
At the sacred name of mother Venus!

III

If only lost time would return!
—Man is done for, has played his part.
In the light, weary of smashing his idols
He revives, free from his Gods,
And, as if he were from heaven, searches the
    skies!
The idea of an invincible, eternal Ideal,
The god who endures within clayey flesh,
Will rise and rise until he burns his brow.
And when you see him sound the horizon,
Shrugging off old yokes, free from fear,
You will offer him divine Redemption!
—Splendid, radiant in the bosom of endless
    oceans
You will rise, releasing infinite love across
An expanding universe with an infinite smile!
The World will quiver like an enormous lyre
In the tremblings of an enormous kiss!

—The World thirsts for love: you slake it.

IV

The splendour of flesh! The splendour of the
    Ideal!
The renewal of love, a triumphant dawn
When, Gods and Heroes kneeling at their feet,

White Callipyge and little Eros
Blanketed in a snow of roses,
Will lightly touch women and flowers
Blossoming beneath their beautiful feet!
O great Ariadne whose tears water
The shoreline at the sight of Theseus' sail,
White in sun and wind. O sweet virgin
By a single night undone, be silent!
Lysios in his golden chariot embroidered
With black grapes, strolling in the Phrygian fields
Among wanton tigers and russet panthers,
Reddens the moss along blue rivers.
Zeus, the Bull, cradles the naked, childlike body
    of Europa
Around his neck as she throws a white arm
Around the God's sinewy shoulders, trembling
    in a wave,
He slowly turns his bottomless stare upon her;
Her pale cheek brushes his brow like a blossom;
Her eyes close; she dies
In a divine kiss; and the murmuring wave's
Golden spume blossoms through her hair.
—Through oleander and lotus
Lovingly glides the great dreaming Swan
Enfolding Leda in the whiteness of his wing;

—And while Cypris, so strangely lovely, passes,

And, arching her richly rounded hips,

Proudly bares her large golden breasts

And her snow white belly embroidered with dark moss,

Hercules—Tamer of Beasts, who as if with a nimbus

Girds his powerful form with a lion skin, his face

Both terrible and kind—heads for the horizon!

In the muted light of the summer moon,

Standing naked and dreaming in the gilded pallor

Staining the heavy wave of her long blue hair,

In the dark clearing where the moss is stung with stars,

The Dryad stares at the silent sky . . .

—White Selene floats her veil

Timidly across the feet of fair Endymion,

And sends him a kiss in a pale beam of light . . .

—The distant Spring weeps in endless ecstasy . . .

Our Nymph, elbow on her urn, dreams

Of the fair white lad her wave had touched.

—A breeze of love passed in the night,

And in the sacred woods, surrounded

By terrible trees, majestic marble forms,

Gods whose brows the Bullfinch makes his nest,
—Gods watch over Man and the unending
Earth.

O our lost paradise.—The grief of Trakl, Rimbaud and Heine springs from the same root as their yearning: horror at bourgeois society, disenchantment as it degrades nature to technology and all human relationships to exchange value—the earth is both dehumanized and de-deified in the triumphal march of the mechanized world and the rationality of profit. The nymphs have left the golden woods, the gods go into exile and human beings are sad and dulled, their heavens clouded. The only old god to die was the immortal Pan, in the days of Emperor Tiberias, when another god's star shone out;[41] now he is not the only one but the first.—We are familiar with Marx's words on disenchantment: 'Is Achilles possible with powder and lead? Or the *Iliad* with the printing press, not to mention the printing machine? Do not the song and the saga and the muse necessarily come to an end with the printer's bar . . . ?'[42] But it can be no coincidence that Heine's account of the great Pan's death comes between those two statements beginning with 'I am', between resignation and revolt. Negation negates itself; knowledge is the passage from despair to hope, and so long as humans are not automata, the old gods are brought to life again, if only by one person's gaze: for E. T. A. Hoffmann in tenements, behind bronze nameplates; for Kafka down by the harbour in the evening; for Anna Seghers perched atop a hoisting crane; and for Rimbaud Pan's hitherto-unknown son emerges from the stone of some museum.

Arthur Rimbaud, 'Antique'

> Graceful son of Pan! Beneath your flower- and berry-crowned brow, the precious spheres of your eyes revolve. Your wine-stained cheeks seem hollow. Your fangs gleam. Your chest is a lyre, music flows from your pale arms. Your heart beats in a belly where two sexes sleep. At night, wander, softly moving this thigh, then this other thigh, and this left leg.[43]

Readers may rediscover this human awakening in Trakl's 'Helian': *Lovely is man, appearing in the dark, / As he moves his arms and legs in wonder / And his eyes roll silent in purple hollows*. We can go into the myth no further here, gladly referring readers to Walter Killy's disquisition.[44] But while in Helian's beautiful garden the *son of Pan* always *sleeps . . . in the grey marble*, in 'Psalm' he enters the human world in the flesh: *The son of Pan appears in the shape of a ditch-digger, / Sleeping through the noon on the smouldering asphalt*. Today these lines are precious to us, and it is hard to grasp that for so long we failed to see them, reading around them, in fact, with a sort of guilty conscience: when you finally find the figure of a working man in Trakl, he's lying there, sleeping in broad daylight!—But he is the son of Pan, the midday sleeper, and his sleep is the shepherd of a humanity that preserves the ancient magic as it dreams.

This merging of worker, dream and myth returns in a line that shocked us: *O myths cooped up in factories' grim grey!*—This line comes in the first draft of a poem which Trakl, as so often, split into myriad versions: 'On the Way' (only vaguely related to a poem of the same title published in *Sebastian Dreaming*[45]):

A scent of incense astray in the dusk.
Fumes submerge squares red and barren.
Bazars are a-whirl, and a gold ray glides
Through old shops so strange and confused.

Decay glows in the dishwater; the wind
Dully wakes the anguish of burnt gardens.
Obsessive minds chase down their golden
*   dreams.*
At windows dryads idle slim and mild.

The dream-sick wander, gnawed by some desire.
Workers glimmer, streaming through a gate.
At sky's edge steel towers loom aglow.
O myths cooped up in factories' grim grey!

An old man minces doll-like in the dark.
A tinkling clink of gold coin lewdly laughs.
A halo's cast around the little girl
Who waits by the cafe, gentle and white.

[...]

Streets bluster, filled with poverty and stench.
Viola hues and harmonies waft past
The hungry huddled in their basement cells.
A lovely child sits dead upon a bench.

The pale children's dance of death; and the son of Pan
sleeps on the smouldering asphalt.—Dryads are tree
nymphs, young women, dwellers in the ancient woods.—
In the second version of 'On the Way', the fairy tale is
already obliterated, for the third stanza has become:

A boy's smile, consumed by some desire.
An old church portal stares, locked up.
Sonatas are heard by well-disposed ears.
A rider trots past on a white horse.

The dream-sick have merged into the figure of the boy,
the open gate of the factory hall shuts as an old church
door, no more glimmering procession, no glow of dawn
that stands for technical progress, and the myth is locked
out at the cost of a weak, clichéd image: the ears well-
disposed to the sonatas, the rider on the white horse. This
obliterates the unity as well; the stanza falls apart into
four separate lines. For Trakl to surrender to poetic
helplessness, he must have needed to obliterate this
vision, but now that we know the discarded version, it
seems preserved in the sleep to which the son of Pan surrenders on the smouldering asphalt.—In this sleep all the

future dreams and all the past reposes.—A glimmer-rain falls before this sleep, and we do not know whether it fecundates, sears or conjures up a Fata Morgana (sometimes we even saw it as the glimmering of the movie screen, and indeed Trakl's 'Psalm' has something very film-like)—it was as a glimmering rain that Zeus spilt himself into Danae's lap through a chink in the dungeon where the wanton woman was buried away by her father, and this encounter engendered Perseus, decapitator of snake-haired Medusa, from whose bloody skull emerged a glimmering gold warrior and Pegasus, the winged steed of the poets.—Does this make too much of half a line? Ah, but: *In his grave the white magician is playing with his serpents*—thus does the poet play with his myths, even if he does not know it: *The soul listens gladly to the white magician's fairy tales.*

But we don't want to digress; we want to tell the reader at long last that this son of Pan, the ditch-digger —and we took this word entirely in its primal sense as a mover of the earth, for that is how a word in poetry is to be taken, a *Wort* with the plural *Worte*—that this son of Pan cast a glimmering light on the figure of the madman. At first a mere thematic connection—Pan is the god who causes madness by frightening wanderers with his laughter, Pan is the god whose death is attested to; so couldn't the god's madness and death merge in one form: *The madman has died*? A legitimate method of poetry and dreams and thus, too, of the attempt to understand; though such constructions often turn brittle quite quickly, this one unexpectedly held up.—Was the madman Pan himself?—That would be too much and too fixed, but he was the one who had to die so that the son of Pan could appear, sleeping on the smouldering asphalt.

All at once the poem displayed a chronological logic: the madman has died; the stranger is buried; a glimmer-rain; the son of Pan.—The madness of the dead man, set between the room whitewashed with milk[46] and the island in the South Sea, now appeared to us as a separating interlude and the madman's death as the gate into the future that is the return of the past. Yet even as this interpretation gripped us so powerfully that we took it as the definitive solution, it turned suspect once again, not only since it contradicted the figure of Pan but also since the madman's death seemed so compellingly to belong to the first part of the stanza, in which everything was one great extinction: the extinguished light, the abandoning of the moorland inn, the burnt vineyard, the spilt milk.—Wasn't one key element of antiquity the veneration of madness as a divine emanation? Weren't madness and poetry inseparable? Wasn't Pan a harbinger of the god of madness, Dionysus? And wasn't madness, in Trakl, always a state that stood in positive contrast to the common sense of his despised bourgeois routine, as his realm of the dead did to that of the living? The poem suddenly acquired historical logic, now that the madman's death stood as an in-between zone bridging past and present.

But hardly was this insight gained than it lost out to the one just discarded which now, and yet again, seemed the only convincing one, and so, in ever-quicker leaps, the meaning of madness switched between salvation and perdition in the in-between zone of separative connection and connective separation; and if just before we had seen him as the black spiders' lord, now he appeared in the circle dance of the swaying women, until these exclusivities came together as poles of the contradiction that is *madness*. And now it seemed conclusive that the *madness* here was poetry itself, that sacred, wicked dowry that so often makes its recipients wish it would die at last, the despised one, and abide for ever, the beloved.

Yet that did not add up either; after all, the words were *The madman has died*,[47] a fact of irretrievability. But the existence of poetry, even in dark times, could not be doubted; or could it? Were these words perhaps a wishful dream? For a moment we saw them as concerning Trakl's own person—had he ever thought of suicide? We did not know; so far we'd wanted no image of a poet; now, suddenly, we were overcome by the desire to know his life and understand this passage: definitively, unequivocally, absolutely.

We found Trakl's biography, a slender volume with an ugly, grey-brown library binding, and felt a strange shock as we opened it: there, in an obliging camera pose, knitted cap covering his ears, stood an awkward, almost unwieldy man; and as we quickly turned the page, we felt a different shock: staring out bare-necked, gross, brutal and depraved from inside an oval hollow was, clearly, a mad murderer: Georg Trakl.

5.

I read this book[48] in a single night, experiencing, to paraphrase Stephan Hermlin,[49] the biography of an unliveable life: an existence that fell to poetry.—An existence that fell to drugs and incest; a fall into decay, a plunge into suicide; a life at the zenith of European poetry.— That night all my delight and torment in Trakl converged; revelations, like a light that bedarkens, smote and bewildered and stunned me: reading mingled with dream.—A sallow brown, the dull gleam of medicine vials, the creak of the club chair's black leather, and from the realm of drugs and delusions a man in a yellow-braided hussar's jacket emerged to tell me unheard-of things: Trakl had worked in a ministry; Trakl had volunteered for the colonial service in Borneo; Trakl had wanted to go to Albania.—Today it takes little effort to ascertain this life's outward events; at the time, in the mid-1960s, little of it was known here.

The best thing I can do is briefly recapitulate how I experienced this life.

Though commonalities were few, from the start, the experience was coloured by a distant familiarity; I thought back to my childhood. Even Salzburg, the city of Trakl's birth, woke memories of a family trip to

Austria—I saw a plate of *Salzburger Nockerln*, a sweet gold-brown soufflé, incredibly filling (even before the trip we'd looked forward to this famous dish, sum of our knowledge of Salzburg, and it surpassed our expectations); I saw the fiacre and the onrush of green-aproned porters descending upon our luggage and the trick fountains of Schloss Hellbrunn, hammering marionettes behind drifting veils of water, but no landscape came to mind. I recalled a scarlet altar boy, lost in the middle of a vast square, but that, no doubt, was already imagined; and then, hewn into the rock of a cliff face, the glimmer of a dungeon: bars, a bundle of straw, a pitcher of water, a prisoner in a hair shirt, gawking onlookers and the nagging certainty that this diorama revealed some lived experience.

Salzburg, then, was where he was born, in 1887; my father was born a year earlier, in a town I didn't know, Brüx, now called Most.—At that moment I would have given a great deal to wander the house of Trakl's birth; in the book I saw a dark courtyard, rugged cobblestones, strange arcades on the upper floors, windows and doors shadowed by arches and everything eerily uninhabited— a Mozart sonata, and Bluebeard's chamber; I did not know then that Trakl had written a play about Bluebeard.—Whither was I straying, at the very start of the way?—I read greedily, yet very slowly: Salzburg, then, in 1887, Waagplatz 2, a bourgeois house; his father, Tobias Trakl, a hardware merchant, prosperous and respectable like my father; I pictured him having his morning pint, behind the shop counter, talking politics, had he also called for hanging the Reds by their heels over smouldering fires?—He was seen as an upright, good-natured man; so was my father.—*Under oak trees we sway on a silver barge.*—Trakl's mother Maria, née Halik, of Czech stock, an artistic woman but queer, withdrawn, oddly forbidding; she never reminded me of my mother, and remained a remote figure. She bore six children: Gustav, Maria, Hermine, Georg, Friedrich, Margarethe; from the father's first marriage there was a half-brother Wilhelm, a well-travelled, experienced businessman.—A ten-room flat, a garden to romp in, servants, a French governess, sailor suits, piano lessons, the peal of bells from a hundred churches and the whorehouse just around the corner.

A sheltered childhood, as they say—I had glimpsed it so often in Trakl's verses: *Childhood's dark stillness. Under budding ash-trees / Gentleness grazes, casting its blue gaze; golden repose*—I reread these lines and read as well this childhood's other side: *A dark thing thrills to the violet's scent; swaying grain / In the dusk, seed and the golden shadows of sadness.*—A sheltered childhood in a lovely garden, yet a childhood like many others, at root a childhood like any, dark stillness and the shadows of sadness, the only question being what will grow from it.—His brother Gustav becomes, what else, a merchant; half-brother Wilhelm already is one;

brother Fritz becomes an officer; Georg is bad at school, so bad, so uninterested in the material that ultimately the only chance for a socially acceptable, skilled profession is to study pharmaceutics which does not require a secondary-school degree: his tenth-grade education qualifies him for a reduced term of military service as a 'one-year volunteer'.

And so Trakl becomes a pharmacist, working at the pharmacy Zum Weissen Engel under Carl Hinterhuber; at this point he has already begun writing poems, turgid, humidly conventional constructions with barely a hint of what is to come; he belongs to a circle of poets called 'Apollo' and has, with the typical *succès d'estime*, tried his hand as a playwright at the Salzburg Municipal Theatre and as a columnist and critic for a local newspaper (he destroyed the two one-act plays that were performed, along with all the reviews, and there is no need to share the other products of those years); he's begun to read modern writers, Baudelaire, Verlaine, Maeterlinck, Dostoevsky, Nietzsche, George, Hofmannsthal, Schnitzler, Kraus, Wilde, Huysmans, Strindberg, Ibsen (Rimbaud, in K. L. Ammer's translation, comes two years later with explosive effect, as do the rediscovered late works of Hölderlin in Trakl's last two years); he is a regular customer at the brothel on Judengasse and has already discovered narcotics, ether and opium cigarettes; now his boss is a drunkard, the realm of drugs has opened wide and poetry works like fate: twilight and decay.—*Damn you dark drugs, / White sleep! / This passing strange garden / Of darkling trees / Filled with serpents, hawkmoths, / Spiders and bats.* This poem's first version began: *Take heart, you dark drugs*—the poles of a unity of contradiction, between them the span and strain of his existence.

What should I tell of this life, of which I learnt one black night long, in a hundred details, that it was unliveable?—Apprenticeship, studies, military service and one unbroken chain of failed professional forays; his profession won't allow him to write as he needs to—constantly—and he can't write without a profession, he needs something to live on, and wine and whorehouses cost money. At first he cares little, but in 1910 Tobias Trakl dies and Georg's half-brother Wilhelm takes over the business, which now, God knows why, takes a sudden downturn and in 1913 is stricken off the commercial register. Hardship, though not catastrophe; Trakl does not suffer penury like his existential archetype Rimbaud, he just can't make ends meet, not with his salary, when he draws one (constantly changing jobs, he usually works as a probationer, unpaid) and certainly not with subsidies.—Ludwig von Ficker and his brother Rudolf support him.—Constant petty embarrassments, constant borrowing, constant debts, all so terribly banal and so terribly humiliating: *All of it, God, so unspeakable, it brings you to your knees.*—The poem in which this line appears tells of everyday, fortifying things; it is called 'On the Way'.—On the way to what? All you sense is this: *All roads end in black putrefaction.*—From a letter to Ludwig von Ficker, dated 11 November 1913: *My affairs are utterly unsettled. Just now I slept for two days and two nights and still have a bad case of Veronal poisoning. In my perplexity and all the despair of late I have no idea how to go on living. I've met obliging people here, but it seems to me they are unable to help me and all will end in darkness.*—From a letter to the poet Karl Borromäus Heinrich, two months later: *Straying from gloom to drunkenness, I lack the strength and inclination to alter a situation that grows more calamitous by the day, leaving only the wish that a storm might descend and cleanse me or destroy me. O God, what guilt and darkness we must pass through. May we manage to endure in the end.*— Between these two letters comes an outburst, in a letter to Ludwig von Ficker, presumably from the end of November 1913: [. . .] *I am at an utter loss. It (is) such a nameless misfortune when one's world breaks asunder. O God, what a judgement has descended upon me. Tell me that I must have the strength to go on living and do what is true. Tell me that I am not mad. A stony darkness has descended. O my friend, how small and miserable I've become . . .*

In five sentences, the fateful word 'descend' comes three times. Trakl's biographers puzzle over the circumstances of this cri de coeur which he never explains; citing an allusion by Ludwig von Ficker, they posit a connection with the pregnancy of his sister Grete, recently married in Berlin,[50] with whom love had united him since childhood, love in the sense that man and woman shall become one flesh; they speak of Trakl's secret, and surely his secret lies hidden here too or, rather, here it seeks the light like the magma of the earth's core in a wound of the rock. But even that night it seemed to me that this secret reposed in the everyday and what was unspeakable was its banality.—To be unable to live your life and yet forced to live it, is that not boundless and hopeless enough, and wouldn't this awareness alone present itself as the realization of inexpiable guilt?—Incest only added to it.—What dawned on me then, in that black night, ineluctable as a nightmare, was how you die daily of an unliveable daily life, the endless banality that grinds you down, leaches you out, eats you up.—Those who experience this capitulation do so in their own way, and those who have not will never understand it.—This is how Kleist died, and Hölderlin, Jakob Lenz, Karoline Günderrode, Christian Dietrich Grabbe, Adalbert Stifter; one of the unknown ones was Christa T.—Well, what of it; the guy should have gone to work instead of racking up debts over those silly little poems—that's true, he says so himself, only he *can't* do any differently, that's why he's an artist, he bears the guilt.—Precisely because it was all so banal I grasped, disconcertingly, the connection between 'guilt' and 'debt' as liability and suddenly, I don't know why, I recalled the first words of Western philosophy which had always tormented me to the point of anguish: 'The things from which existing things come into being are also the things into which they are destroyed, in accordance with what must be. For they give justice and reparation to one another for their injustice in accordance with the ordering of time.'[51]— Later I would find an echo of Anaximander in Trakl's parting words before his journey into suicide. 'Your poem does not expiate your guilt!'

I had not yet discovered the three-volume diaries of Karl Röck, an Innsbruck municipal officer who jotted down his encounters with Trakl beginning summer 1912; his notes attest quite well to the banality but never grasp the deadly humiliation:

> Tues, 20 Aug. at MAX (borrowed 30 crowns from Fi for evening with Kr) [. . .] Evening. Theresia; Trakl comes drunk, screaming like a child. [. . .] (Spitting); talk of the dying light bulb in the light well. Then I and Trakl go to Lehner. He reads 'The Rats' to me (and 'Melancholy'). Talk of his father's watch strap he pawned and spent on whores.

> Sat, 4 Apr. Trakl back from Berlin w. severe overdose, led by the arm; Fi, E, I go to Rose, Trakl reads 'Occident'.

> 1 May. Trakl borrowed 10 crowns at MAX.

> 13 May. Lent Trakl 20 crowns.

Tues, 19 May. Fi's wife complains about all the drugs Trakl's taking, says today they kept him in bed till evening again.

26 Oct. Trakl needs 200 crowns a month: 2 crowns a day for drinking wine and smoking. How many people *live* on that amount of money.[52]

So it goes, on and on, dates unimportant, no progress: twilight and decay.

In the twilight both craving and fearing the night, submitting to decay and resisting it, Trakl tries to establish a livelihood but aborts the attempt again and again; when employed by the Ministry of Public Works in Vienna, for example, he does so after spending just two hours in the office, which he uses to write his resignation. The precise course of events is immaterial; the upshot is recorded in Röck's diary:

4 Jan. (1913) Trakl picks me up from the office at 6, reads out his new poem 'Helian' at my place. Just from listening I only picked up details, not the whole, and I told him that. I would have to read it first. Told movingly, even harrowingly of his new job in Vienna, where he was utterly preoccupied with his 'Helian' in the days before New Year's. That's why he fled from the job. Evening. Trakl and I invited to Fi. Trakl is living in Fi's loggia room.

Unliveable life, so it went: after his military service Trakl applies for a trainee position at the Ministry of Public Works, works a while longer at the Weisser Engel while waiting for a response, goes back to the army, works on a trial basis at the garrison infirmary in Innsbruck, hands in his resignation shortly after receiving a permanent position, as he's now been accepted by the Ministry, works at the Ministry for two hours and resigns, applies for a position as a pharmaceutical officer at the War Ministry, is accepted, asked to check columns of figures, despairs at the task, reports sick and resigns, contemplates returning to the army again, contemplates reapplying to the Ministry of Public Works, puts out feelers to Viennese hospitals and retracts them as soon as they touch Vienna, applies to the Dutch colonial service as a military pharmacist and also for a job as a military pharmacist in the mountains of Albania. Rimbaud's wayfaring life is the model at hand and yet—excepting one short trip to Berlin and one to Venice and an excursion to Lake Garda—Trakl fails to escape his narrow circuit. —He can no longer bear it; now his lovely homeland turns into the crater of Aden in which Rimbaud found his hell: *There is a vineyard, burnt and black with holes full of spiders. / There is a room, and they've white-washed it with milk.*—When will the madman die at last? Or—it is the same thing—when will they cease to white-wash cloacae with milk?—*I yearn for the day when the soul will no longer be willing and able to dwell in this ill-fated body with its pestilence of gloom, when it will depart this mockery of a form made from dung and rot, an all-to-true reflection of a godless, cursed century.* (Letter to Ludwig von Ficker, June 1913)—In late June 1914 Adolph Loos, the famous architect, countered: 'Regard yourself as a vessel of the Holy Spirit which no one, not even Georg Trakl, may destroy.'—But what if the Holy Spirit itself destroys this vessel and *is* the Holy Spirit by very virtue of having to destroy it?—*O the flute of light; O the flute of death.*

His haunts are abhorrent, ruined for him: *this gutter full of mendacity and meanness repels me*—what once held for the detail now holds for the whole.—He calls Salzburg a *town gone to rot*; Innsbruck the *meanest and most brutal town . . . that ever existed on this burdened and cursed earth*; Vienna is *this filthy town*; every town is a filthy town: *Maybe I will go to Borneo!*[53]—Rimbaud simply went; of course he, at the age of eighteen, had already finished his poem for the moment; singular things do not repeat.—And Rimbaud did not experience what Trakl did: Ludwig Wittgenstein, at the time an industrial tycoon—later, as a world-famous philosopher, he would be destitute himself—remits an enormous sum to Ficker for the support of struggling talents; Trakl (and likewise Rilke) is to receive 20,000 crowns.[54] That would relieve his financial troubles for years but the beneficiary is unable to cash in the bequest: outside the bank he begins to tremble and can't bring himself to cross the threshold. Fear of others, unspeakably foolish, but it is such foolishness that wrecks him.—Should society be blamed for that?—The Viennese writer Franz Zeis wrote to his wife-to-be:

> Vienna, 17 July 1913 . . . I was with Trakl Sunday, Monday and yesterday . . . He is a sweet-natured person, taciturn, withdrawn, shy, utterly intro-verted. Looks strong, sturdy, but he's sensitive and ill. Has hallucinations, 'raves' (says Schwab[55]). Now and then, trying to express some mysterious thing, he has such a tormented way of speaking, holding his hands, palms up, at shoulder height, fingers curled, cramped, head slightly tilted, shoulders slightly raised, eyes fixed on you ques-tioningly. On trains, for example, he can't sit, never, he can't tolerate having someone across from him. He always stands in the corridor, even on hour-long journeys, even at night. He can't use the telephone, he simply can't . . .

His childhood friend Erhard Buschbeck reported that as a 'rezeptuarius' at the Weisser Engel, Trakl went through six shirts in a single afternoon, sweating for fear of the customers.—What did my father quip? 'Daft Georgie!'

How many must have seen him as Schwab did? For his first collection of poems to be published (by Kurt Wolff, Leipzig, after being rejected by Albert Langen in Munich), friends drummed up subscriptions for it, partly through advertisements in *Die Fackel* and *Der Brenner*, which had printed Trakl's poems regularly since May 1912; around a hundred people signed up, most of them probably won over by Dr Schwab or Paula von Ficker:[56] 'Yesterday Ludwig read me an utterly insane postcard from Trakl. I wouldn't give him any more money, let him ask Ludwig if he needs some. These people never leave you in peace . . . '—How true!—Trakl's card, undated as always, postmarked 12 November 1913, reads: *Dear Herr von Ficker! Please make this final change to the last line of the Kaspar Hauser Song to read as follows: 'As that of one unborn the stranger's red head sank' (one line). Loos asks me to dedicate the poem to his wife. So please add this dedication: for Bessie Loos. Finally, I ask that you send me the proofs as soon as possible. Many greetings to your dear children. Of late I have consumed a sea of wine, schnapps and beer. Sober. Greet Röck and Esterle as well. Your very devoted Georg Trakl.—Corr. line 1: Verily he loved the sun that climbed purple down the hill. Line 1 of the first stanza remains unchanged, i.e.: 'earnest'.*

To fully appreciate what Paula von Ficker described as 'utterly insane', it is necessary to add that this card was preceded by one the day before, also concerning corrections to the 'Kaspar Hauser Song' and reading as follows: [. . .] *Dear friend, would you make the following change to the Kaspar Hauser Song: Line 1: He loved the sun that went purple down the hill—Stanza 2 line 1 'truthful' instead of 'earnest'—Last line: Silver sank*

the head of one unborn.—p.s. please let me know
whether you have made the corrections. Many greetings
from Kraus and Loos. I kiss your dear wife's hand.

First 'earnest', then 'truthful', then 'earnest' again: it
is the shift between being and wanting, between the
object and subject of the story, with the responsibility
remaining unchanged. A difficult choice: a unity of contradiction, with the emphasis finally placed on the
subject.—It was the choice between liability and liability:
earnest or *truthful*; quite a decision.

Trakl revised constantly, even as the book was going
to press: barely a letter, even in extremities of anguish,
failed to contain such a request and the demand for
confirmation.—He wrote on whatever came to hand:
envelopes, menus, letters, documents; the 'Kaspar Hauser
Song', for example, is written on letterhead from the
Brenner Verlag in Innsbruck.—Though his handwriting
is generally legible, all the corrections and counter-
corrections and re-corrections sometimes render his
manuscripts indecipherable: the lines flow into one
another, branch out and join once more; his *oeuvre* is
ultimately one single poem.—Kaspar Hauser was a
strange foundling, a boy ignorant of reading and writing
—and life—and feral to the verge of animality, who at
Whitsun 1828 suddenly appeared at the home of a
Nuremberg cavalry captain with a letter in his hand and
was murdered a year later; he is reported to have said
that he wanted to become a cavalryman; his origins and

his murder remain unclarified.—Verlaine put him in a poem; Trakl must have seen a reflection of himself.— *Earnest was his dwelling in the shade of the tree / And pure was his face.*—A glimpse of the future that is denied: O our lost paradise.

In the last two years of his life Trakl was always welcome in Ludwig von Ficker's villa in Mühlau on the outskirts of Innsbruck and Rudolf von Ficker's Schloss Hohenburg near Igls; there, in almost total seclusion, he lived out all that was granted him: writing.—*Tell me that I must have the strength to go on living and do what is true.*—So terribly banal; so terribly humiliating.

The Swiss writer Hans Limbach gave an account of Trakl's daily life in Mühlau; here is the part that immediately concerns Trakl:

> I had noted Trakl's poems in *Der Brenner* but had not yet found a way to relate to them, though several lines in the 'Psalm' and, perhaps more so, the response by Karl Kraus[57] had impressed me. It was the portrait drawing by Max von Esterle that first sparked my keen interest. Now F. showed us a strange self-portrait which Trakl had painted at that painter's studio, having come straight there from the train station on returning from his sister's sickbed in Berlin, a pale mask with three holes—eyes and mouth.
>
> At that moment Trakl himself walked into the room.

Standing up, he seemed shorter and stockier than when seated. Without any sign of pleasure, merely murmuring a greeting, he shook our hands and sat down.

His features were coarse, like a worker's, an impression heightened by his short neck and slovenly clothing—he did not wear a collar, his shirt fastened only by a button. All the same, his figure radiated an incredible dignity. But a dark, almost malicious streak lent him the fascination of a criminal. For in truth his face stared like a mask: his mouth barely opened when he spoke, only his eyes sometimes glittered uncannily.

D.,[58] in his ingenuous fashion, immediately assailed him with questions; but Trakl responded tersely, as though reluctant, and when one of the questions seemed to hit too close for comfort, he drew back, shy and almost hostile.

Then we were asked in to dinner.

After dinner we returned to the study, taking wine and glasses with us.

Only now, under the influence of the wine, did Trakl gradually come alive. He no longer recoiled so sensitively at D.'s questions; more and more often, in a quiet voice that rumbled like distant thunder, he tossed out sibylline, oracular words and phrases which in their striking imagery suddenly gave me the key to his poems: in a sense he wrote exactly as he spoke.

D.'s open, slightly childish nature seemed to irritate and provoke Trakl; to all appearances it embarrassed him to be interrogated, and D. did not seem sufficiently conscious of that.

Trakl's essence was profound reticence. 'I'm only half born!' he said at one point, claiming that up to his twentieth year he had noticed nothing whatsoever of the world around him but *water*. The autobiographical sketch 'Dream and Derangement' which he wrote at that very time wonderfully conveys this vague, tormented state.

But D. clearly lacked any feeling for his nature and kept pressing him.

'Are you familiar with Walt Whitman?' he asked him suddenly.

Trakl said he did but added that he thought him a corrupting influence.

'Why?'—D. burst out—'Why corrupting? Don't you appreciate him? Surely you have a certain kinship with him in your own way?'

F. observed that if anything one saw a profound antagonism between the two, for Whitman simply affirmed life in all its manifestations while Trakl was a pessimist through and through.

So didn't he have any pleasure in life?—D. pressed on.—Didn't his work give him any satisfaction, for example?

'It does,'—Trakl admitted—'but one must be wary of this satisfaction.'

D. leant back in sheer astonishment.

'So why don't you just join a monastery?' he asked at last after a brief silence.

'I'm a Protestant,' Trakl replied in a strained voice.

'A Pro-te-stant?' D. drew out the word.—'I never would have guessed!—But then you ought at least to live in the country, not the city, to be far from the madding crowd and closer to nature!'

'I have no right to escape from Hell,' Trakl rejoined.

'But Christ escaped from it too!'

'Christ is the Son of God!' Trakl replied.

D. could hardly contain himself.

'So you also believe that all salvation comes from him? You take the words "Son of God" in the literal sense?'

'I am a Christian,'—Trakl replied.

'Well,'—the other man continued, 'how do you explain such unchristian figures as the Buddha or the Chinese sages?'

'They too have received their light from Christ.'

We fell silent, reflecting on the profundity of this paradox. But D. would not leave well enough alone.

'And the Greeks? Don't you also believe that mankind has sunk much lower since then?'

'Never has mankind sunk so low as now, after Christ's manifestation,'—Trakl retorted. 'It *couldn't* sink so low!' he added after a brief pause.

Seemingly refusing to see how Trakl retreated into himself, growing more and more withdrawn, D. produced Nietzsche as his final trump card.

'Nietzsche was mad!'—Trakl blurted out harshly, an uncanny glitter in his eyes.

'How do you mean that?'

'I mean,'—he growled—'that Nietzsche had the same disease as Maupassant!'

His face was terrible as he said this; the demon of falsehood seemed to glitter in his eyes.

'One mustn't say that,' D. admonished him severely, with all the moral authority of truth's champion.—'One mustn't say that! You ought to know that the causes of madness are psychological!'

Trakl, who had bowed his head, looked up, gauged D. with a strange glance and said nothing. But after a while he seemed to recall his words about Christ.

'It is unheard of,'—he began—'how Christ, with the simplest words, solves humanity's most profound problems. Can the question of the communion between man and woman be solved more fully than by the commandment: *They shall become one flesh*?'

D. seemed astonished; after a short silence he remarked: 'Yes, that's it. Maybe one day I can aspire to a marriage in that spirit.'

From a man of nearly fifty who had gone through several unhappy marriages, there was something touching, even wonderful about this statement.

In the meantime the wine bottles had been emptied and as no more wine could be found in the kitchen, Trakl, without much ado, took the bottles under his arm, descended into the cellar like an innkeeper and brought them back refilled.

The rest of the evening unfolded quietly. Several times already Trakl had regarded me silently. Now he asked me about Russia and his deep sympathy for its people came to light.

Dostoevsky was especially dear to his heart. He spoke of several characters, such as Alyosha Karamazov and Sonya from *Crime and Punishment*, with profound feeling.

As far as I recall, speaking of Sonya he made the fine statement—again with wildly glittering eyes: 'The dogs who claim that woman seeks only sensual pleasure ought to be struck dead! Woman seeks *the justice that is hers*, just as any of us do!'

He also spoke of Tolstoy with great veneration: 'Pan collapsing beneath the cross,' he called him.

As we parted, I looked gravely into his eyes. Something like distant lightning flared in them quickly and then faded. But I knew he had taken kindly to me. [59]

This encounter took place in January or February 1914; at the end of March, Trakl travelled to see his sister Grete in Berlin and returned utterly distraught; he applied for a post as a military pharmacist in the Dutch foreign service and in the newly founded state of Albania, fantastic plans, doomed to failure, what remained for him?—Crushing guilt.—In Berlin, Trakl met Else Lasker-Schüler; she wrote him two letters, saying in the last one: '[I]f you go on drinking, I'll break my oath and start drinking again. Tirol must be so beautiful, I'd love to see it myself some day; I'll get drunk there on green or on the fire of the lightning bolts . . . '—After his death she wrote him a poem in memoriam; he dedicated his 'Occident' to her:

> *You great cities*
> *Erected stony*
> *On the plain!*
> *How mutely*
> *The exile*
> *With his dark brow follows*
> *The wind, the hill's bare trees.*
> *You rivers that glimmer from afar!*
> *Great is the alarm*
> *Of evening's awful glow*
> *In the storm clouds.*
> *You dying peoples!*
> *Pale wave*
> *Shattering on night's shore,*
> *Falling stars.*

—The war had not yet come.

Of his correspondence with his youngest sister, only one letter, from Grete, has survived; the family destroyed the documents, ashamed of them, no doubt.—One single letter of indeterminate date: in great distress Grete asks her brother, penniless himself, to obtain money for her; we do not know whether he succeeded.—Grete, like Georg, was a drug addict; when he came to visit her, she was bed-bound, suffering from the effects of a late abortion; three years after her brother's death, she put an end to her own life.—Trakl wrote from Berlin to Ludwig von Ficker: *My poor sister is still suffering greatly. Her life is one of such heart-rending sadness and yet such upright courage that it sometimes makes me feel very small; and she, a thousand times more than I, would deserve to live among good, noble people, as was granted me to such an extraordinary degree in a difficult time.*

How might this life have gone on?—We know only that it was unliveable.—The World War broke out; did it come as a deliverance? It was seen that way by millions.—Trakl cannot have succumbed to the sludge-wave of jingoism that deluged Europe like Atlantis; his affinity for the Russian people and his aversion towards Teutonia are well attested: *I wish the executioner's axe on every German's head*! This he pronounced with deadly earnest, an execration like that of Vienna and Innsbruck; and those were Austrian cities. —The shared language often obscures the differences between Austrians (likewise the Swiss) and Germans; for the Austrians Germany is a foreign country, and not the best loved.—For Trakl, the Other to the focus of his contempt was the open-hearted humanity described by Tolstoy and Dostoevsky; in 1914, Karl Röck noted in his diary: 'Mon, 10 Aug. afternoon in MAX with Trakl, then told him outside the Town Hall I can't see him as long as the war goes on, can't take his Russophilia now; he: affectionate.'—In a later reminiscence, Röck gave this scene in fuller detail:

[T]hen I said, I have to tell you something, I won't meet with you again as long as the war lasts . . . I can't stand it any longer to hear the Germans spoken of that way. And I myself spoke that way; I myself said it might be better for the Germans if they lost to the Russians, which was sacrilegious lunacy . . . He said he was convinced of it and after all, he didn't *write* it. I: I can't hear such things. I may be forced to think them myself and have thought them. But now that the war has come, how could I say such things? And even if I could: at most to a German who loved the Germans. But not to someone who loves the Russians and what is more: hates the Germans . . . To listen to things like: No greatness will ever come out of Germany again—I can't hear that.

Well, one nationalism is worth just as much as another; no salvation shall come from there, but what cried out from the torment of the mind and heart was not some other nationalism.

And yet the deliverance of a decision came: on 24 August 1914, Trakl embarked with an ambulance corps for Field Hospital 7/14, departing at midnight from Innsbruck's main station; was my father there too? I can no longer ask him, so I'll believe it: alongside daft Georgie, he climbs into the cattle car.—He waves at me; May 1945: We'll meet again after the victory!—Ludwig von Ficker accompanied his friend; he recalled a carnation in Trakl's cap, and his serene face, and that it was a

moonlit night, and that Trakl wrote down an experience for him on a piece of paper: *Feeling in moments
of death-like being: all human beings are worthy of
love. Awakening you feel the bitterness of the world;
therein is all your unresolved guilt; your poem an imperfect expiation.*

One more aphorism has come down to us from
Trakl's pen: *Insight comes only to him who despises
happiness.*

Blind clock-hands climb towards midnight; the train
trundles out.—My father singing, Trakl silent; a silver
moon.—The train trundles eastward.—Of Trakl's brief
war days, as of the rest of his life, there are sparse tidings:
*Tomorrow or the day after we will march onward. A
great new battle seems to be in preparation. May the
heavens have mercy on us this time.*—The Battle of
Grodek.—The two most important outside testimonials
are Ludwig von Ficker's account of his meeting with
Trakl in the Krakow garrison hospital, and the letter by
the miner Mathias Roth who served Trakl as an officer's
orderly; then come the official hospital documents and
three accounts by comrades-in-arms,[60] one of which we
include here, for it seems uniquely suited to convey the
unspeakable. The pharmacologist Heinz Klier wrote the
piece, 'A Military Pharmacist on the Front', published in
the *Salzburger Volksblatt* on 28 December 1914:

> The Battle of Lemberg was underway; we heard
> the rumbling from nearby Grodek. [. . .] And it

was here that I met my first Salzburg acquaintance on the front. It was my colleague Georg Trakl. We cheerfully toasted our chance meeting, exchanged stories and parted with the wish for a happy reunion. Later I met Trakl several more times, the last time, I believe, near Limanowa, where we spent several cheerful days. Soon after that I read the sad news in the *Salzburger Volksblatt* that my colleague Trakl had died the death of a hero. Fiducit![61]

Unspeakable—and *Fiducit!*—The cheerful, clean death of a hero.—My father had no idea; all he knew was that Trakl had suddenly vanished, probably discharged, that daft Georgie, of use for nothing but drinking. —Indeed it seems he was: in the stinking maelstrom as the fall of the supposedly invulnerable Austrian fortress of Przemyśl sucked the poor soldiers to their deaths (in *The Last Days of Mankind*, Karl Kraus captured this ghastly jumble of prestige mania and incompetence with quotes of Medusa-like effect)—in the Battle of Grodek an incident occurred, nothing extraordinary, a little piece of war's routine that one so inclined could interpret as indicating uselessness.—A barn filled with the wounded, trees filled with the hanged, torment and helplessness, screams and curses, the mess of a botched retreat, these were things experienced by millions.—Continuation of peacetime routine by other means.—When my father was in a good mood and felt some character training was called for, he would regale us at lunch with recollections of goings-on back in the field hospital, belief-beggaring hussar escapades of pluck and improvisation, ever-true to the motto: Where there's a will, there's a way! The pièce de résistance of this ingenuity, that is, usefulness, was the depiction of a bladder operation which my father, the untrained surgeon, had performed without anaesthesia in a sugar-beet field; vividly he described the fountains of three days' pent-up urine and the relief in the face of the man thus delivered; perhaps Henry Miller was watching.—Or how, in the Carpathian winter, they spent three days and nights sawing off frozen legs non-stop, pyramids of black feet in the snow, and how they made surgical thread from the guts of slaughtered cats, and how they paused amid piss and pus for ham sandwiches; he was fond of interposing moments of humour, grim cannibalistic jests with culinary elements, but I can't recall a single detail, only his hearty monstrous laughter, good-natured and berserk.—He never spoke of hanged peasants; he won't have paid much attention to them, it was part of the routine: there wasn't a village that was not dominated by a gallows.—He liked to tell of orgiastic extremes, whether in putting away wine or bearing thirst.—He even passed along a little song, 'Shells, dum-dums and shrapnel, dul-yi-öh, that's the greatest fun for me, horr-i-do, shells, dumdums and shrapnel, dul-yi-öh, that's the greatest fun for me!'—Fiducit!—In the war he'd faced the music like a man; it was necessary to face it like a man, and he'd received the Silver Cross of Merit, the certificate hung in his office next to his pharmacist's diploma and his favourite painting: an owl with glowing eyes and a skull and a parchment book.

But what did happen to Trakl, that daft Georgie? In what void had he vanished? All that has been written about Trakl's Galician days and his departure from Field Hospital 7/14—including a novella, no, a 'novella'—is based on the sole authentic account, Ludwig von Ficker's record of his last meeting with Trakl. Let it stand here in its entirety; not a single detail is superfluous:

The next news I received from Trakl was a censored postcard from the front marked 'Krakow, Garrison Hospital No. 15, Ward 5', written by himself:

> *Dear friend! I have spent the past five days here in the garrison hospital while they monitor my mental state. My health appears to be somewhat impaired and I lapse quite often into unutterable melancholy. Hopefully these days of dejection shall soon be past. Many kind regards to your wife and your children. Please wire me a few words. I would be so glad to have news of you. Cordially, your devoted Georg Trakl. Best regards to Röck.*

At this message, which indicated that none of his friends' greetings had reached Trakl at the front, I travelled to Krakow.

I arrived early in the morning on 24 October, a Saturday, and stayed until the following evening. Like the city itself, the reception area of the garrison hospital was in a tumult: Przemyśl had been surrounded on three sides and the enemy was pressing from the north, making the situation precarious.

The head physician, a Czech, seemed distracted as I stated my business and expressed the desire, evidently rather naive, too civilian-minded, to take my ailing friend with me—immediately if possible!—to be cared for at home. He merely shook his head silently, as though to fend me off. But an assistant physician standing nearby, a Pole, took me aside, saying that Trakl was under his treatment and that he was very much interested in his case. Glad to find a sympathetic ear, I told him all that might arouse his professional and human interest, especially emphasizing that depressive states of this kind were no rare occurrence for Trakl and tended to pass over quickly in the right environment. Then I asked for permission to speak to my friend immediately, outside visiting hours, which the doctor granted.

In a corridor on the ground floor of the Psychiatric Clinic I stopped a passing attendant and asked for Trakl. He went to the nearest, black-painted door and opened a peephole: 'Is that the man you mean?'—I glanced inside, 'Thank you—yes!' Trakl sat on the edge of the bed, his blouse loosely buttoned, smoking a cigarette, and seemed to be conversing calmly with someone I could not see at the moment. The cell, narrow and high, was fogged with a fine cigarette haze, but through a high window with heavy crossbars fell a full beam of early morning sun, glinting golden through the cloud of smoke as through gently stirring morning fog. Suddenly, putting away the cigarette, Trakl very slightly turned his head, looking keenly at the door as though meeting my gaze. At that I was already opening the door—and now my friend, having risen to his feet, came towards me calmly, eyes wide, and took me in his arms without a word.

His demeanour seemed in no way altered, and quite composed. When I asked about his health, he said it was tolerable. And it was only by chance that I found him still here; he had been close to leaving the hospital—as he spoke he took a postcard from the bedside table and showed it to me. 'You see, I wrote you about it!' But he hadn't sent the card (which I skimmed and returned to him), because he'd recently come down with a sore throat that forced him to remain for the time being. Now the fever was gone and he had recovered but was surprised to find that the doctors seemed to have dropped the subject of releasing him from this situation. He had the impression that they were stringing him along with excuses.

I tried to dispel his concerns but at the same time felt rather uneasy. I recalled from the conversation with the doctor, who had seen several of Trakl's poems while censoring the post, that he saw this case as an example of 'Genius and Madness', which seemed to imply that further caution and observation would be required.

I was to learn the thrust of Trakl's suspicions in the afternoon, as we strolled in the hospital garden. It was a fine fall day, slightly overcast, and the air was almost spring-like, mild and soft. In his self-possessed fashion, when in each moment he seemed absorbed by recalling the unforgettable, he told me his experiences on the front, so few and yet so fateful for him. His sanitary train had been deployed for the first time in the Battle of Grodek, just before the turning point, as the outbreak of panic at the front was already surging to the rear. In a barn near the town's main square, without any medical assistance, he'd had to care for ninety badly wounded men, powerless, helpless himself, enduring this ordeal for two days. The groans of the sufferers still echoed in his ears, the pleas to put an end to their torment. Suddenly, barely audible in all the moaning, came a faint detonation: a man shot in the bladder had put a bullet through his head and now bloody brain matter clung to the wall. At that Trakl had to go outside. But every time he went out, another horrific sight mesmerized and petrified him. For on the square, one moment swarming with life and then as though swept clean, stood several trees. A group of uncannily motionless trees, from each of which a hanged man dangled. Ruthenians, executed townsmen. One of them, the last to be strung up, had, Trakl learnt (or had he seen it himself?), placed the noose around his own neck. He let the sight sink deep into his mind, he said: Here *all* humanity's misery laid hands upon you! He could never forget that, nor the retreat; nothing was as terrible as a retreat in disarray.

And then—Trakl went on—somewhere one evening, still during the retreat, it had happened. At dinner with his comrades he had suddenly stood up declaring, beset by fear, that he couldn't go on living, he hoped they'd excuse him, but he had to shoot himself, and bolted out; at which his comrades hurried after him and wrested the pistol from his hand as his strength and will and consciousness fled. An awkward incident, he was well aware, that outburst of despair due to which he now found himself here in such an unfortunate situation. For though he had quickly recovered from the attack of weakness and carried on his duties without further distress, fourteen days later, at Limanowa, he had been posted to the garrison hospital in Krakow, not, as he'd supposed, to serve as a pharmacist, but instead—well, I knew it and saw it: there was nothing to be done.

And suddenly Trakl stopped, hands clasped behind his back, sunk in contemplation—in the hospital gown he wore, somehow fatally reminiscent of prisoner's garb, he was the very image of human dignity, a heart-rending sight—and raised his head, giving me an uncertain, questioning look: 'What do you think? You see, I'm afraid they'll court-martial and execute me for that incident. Faint-heartedness, you know: an expression of cowardice in the face of the enemy. I must be prepared for it.' Alarmed, I tried to talk him out of this delusion: 'Not at all, what makes you think that?' 'Oh, yes,' he insisted, 'there've been incidents, it happens. And besides—why else would they be keeping me here?'—Well, as far as that was concerned, I replied, I was convinced that soon I'd be able to get him out of here and take him home to recover, he could rest assured of that. By now the sun had set, it was growing cool and we headed back towards the entrance. He stopped once again before we went inside: 'So—*they won't*? You think: *they won't*?' 'No, my friend, no! What on earth are you thinking!'

He shared his room with a lieutenant from the Windischgrätz dragoons who was suffering from delirium tremens, but in a few days would be taken home on convalescent leave by his father, a landowner in Slovakia. What a demanding comrade this man was, doubly burdensome in such close quarters, but borne by Trakl with touching patience and forbearance for the unfortunate soul—the fits of rage, alternating between naps with accesses of absurdly jovial talkativeness, the foul abuse which he showered, for lack of his own servant, on Trakl's, who had been put at his disposal and could do nothing to please him, abuse which once, in my presence, so enraged the fellow that, trembling all over, he cried out in anguish, pointed to Trakl and gasped out: 'That man there is my master, not you!' At which Trakl, containing himself with an effort, rebuked his comrade, saying: 'Look, I beg you—leave the poor man alone, can't you see he's doing what he can!' On top of that came the commotion, the constant comings and goings outside in the corridor, the brutish attendants, the occasional racket and cries from the lunatics in the upper floors and the overall impression of a prison cell that intensified to the point of desolation as darkness fell. And finally, when night had come: the vulnerability of all abject creatures in this world of senseless violence, an impression unforgettably heightened when Trakl's servant, a pale, sickly-looking man, spread a tarp and a blanket over a small pile of wood wool on the ground and lay down to sleep in the nook between the wall with the window and the head of his master's iron bed: that, then, was the scene of my last encounter with my friend.

The next afternoon I found him lying down; he seemed gloomier than the day before and distant, despite his still-tangible presence of mind.—'Do you want to hear what I wrote on the front?' he asked after a time. 'It's awfully little', he added, as the Windischgrätz dragoon, visibly displeased at my reappearance, turned in bed to face the wall, yawning with boredom. And now, simply speaking the words, in his unique way, he read two poems: 'Lament' and 'Grodek'—the latter, his last, in a version whose conclusion, looking forward to the fate of the unborn grandchildren, was broader in scope, without the sudden foreshortening which seems to refract Trakl's gaze and lift it out of the world.

I was shaken, and though our sleeping companion's snores sawed loud and awkward
through the hush, my friend's sad muteness held
me long in its embrace like an arm that had
fallen asleep.—'Would you like to have it for *Der
Brenner*?' he asked at last. 'Gladly,' I replied,
thanking him.—'When will you print it?'—'In
the spring, I hope, as a yearbook . . . It'll partly
depend on whether the war will be over soon, or
whether I'll be enlisted and sent off myself.'—
'God forbid,' Trakl murmured, then stared ahead
silently. Then he took a booklet from his bedside
table and handed it to me: 'Do you know this
here?' I replied in the negative; it was the poems
of Johann Christian Günther. 'I didn't know him
either,' Trakl remarked, 'but he's worth knowing,
especially for the Germans now. Yes: he deserves
remembering and not forgetting . . . Although,'
he added after musing for a moment, 'yes, it has
to be said—the harshness of some of his verses
is hardly bearable, and hardly fair . . . Allow me!'
He took the booklet from my hand—only the
last leaves had been cut—and opened it: 'These
are the bitterest verses that ever a German poet
wrote—listen!' And he read:

> I fear, I fear the west's aglow,
> And from the north the threat's upon thee.
> Strange folk may reap the fields thou sowst.

I'd spare it thee. Remember me.
Thou mayst expel me, damned and shamed.
Like Bias now I face the flames.
Departing all but fate forswear,
Thy dust kicked up before my feet,
For now I want no more of thee,
Not even this last breath of air.

'It's called "To His Fatherland",' Trakl said after a pause—'that was the last stanza'—and he shook his head. And repeated the last three lines by heart, as though savouring their bitterness to the fullest. Then he took up the booklet once more: 'But the finest and greatest, just listen, is the last: "Thoughts of Penance". You should know that Günther died young, at 27.' And he began:

My God! How comes it that the springtide
of my years
Has slipped away so stealthily, so quickly
disappears?

Now reading the poem's twenty-five stanzas quietly and movingly, with a sober evenness from which, with a touch of melancholy exhilaration, he distinctly elevated the beautiful stanza:

Come now, as you please, to settle ancient
debts;

> That heavy garb of flesh may rend and fall
>   to dust.
> For rotting it attains to new transparency.
> I'll go before it, yearning joyfully,
> And at gravesides find the habit of that
>   slumber
> Which no idle dream shall evermore
>   encumber—

Then continuing with a sigh, his voice subsiding
weakly:

> O gentle resting place, O Elysian Fields!
> You lie before me, Paradise revealed,
> And I stand, I know not how, moved most
>   inwardly . . .

And when he had finished:

> Should ere my sudden fall cast down my
>   body in the dust,
> Let me then while away time and pain upon
>   thy breast,
> And lift in pitying arms the spirit thenceforth
>   free!
> Have I offended anyone, and gone yet unfor-
>   given?
> Then let these words upon his heart and on
>   my grave be written:
> Often a good death is the best biography—

—When he had finished, he seemed exhausted and in need of rest. He closed his eyes. I was sitting on his bed; time passed silently. The sick man on the opposite bed had woken in all his bloated onerousness and lay staring over at us with glassy eyes. Outside the day drew to a close; the shadowy crosses of the window bars, which just now had stretched out on the floor, fading off into the distance, seemed dissolved in twilight; it was dusk and I felt, my God, I know not how. Accidentally my foot jostled a row of empty and full beer bottles that stood under the bed and set them clinking. The world suddenly seemed desolate, but not for a moment, I must admit, did I think this might be farewell. There was something powerful and unfailing in my friend's presence, impossible to imagine the world without, and when he stirred and asked how late it was and whether he'd fallen asleep, I took courage and tried to give the conversation a carefree turn. With little success, as was soon clear. But it did give me an opportunity to ask Trakl casually whether he still had any drugs in his possession. 'Why, of course, as a pharmacist, I ask you,' he replied almost jovially, with a good-natured smile, 'would I still be alive otherwise? Only naturally no one here must know— or else I'd be in a pretty fix!'—Soon after that the doctor poked his head through the door:

'Everything all right?' He was doing his evening round. I followed him into the corridor and implored him once again to see that Trakl would soon be released and sent on convalescent leave, which he, in haste, promised lightly but quite sincerely. I returned to Trakl with this good news. But sighing and withdrawn, he had little interest left in doctors and their promises. When his servant went to fetch dinner—by now it was dark—I felt the time had come to bid my friend farewell. I went up to his bed, collected myself and promised to stop in Vienna on my way back and do all I could from there to hasten his release from the hospital; then we would soon meet again in Innsbruck. 'Do you think so?' he said in a strange, soft voice. 'I—hope so,' I replied, taken aback. Trakl squeezed my hand briefly, thanked me for my visit and asked me to give his regards to his friends. Then he lay back like one who wishes to muse in the dark for a while before going to sleep, and pulled up his blanket. When I turned back from the door, the room was already so dark that I could barely see his face. I nodded at him once more, unthinkingly taking a few steps back towards him, and: 'Farewell, my dear friend! May we meet again soon!' I said as though in a dream.

Trakl lay motionless and said not a word.

Just gazed at me.

Gazed after me . . .

Never will I forget that look.[62]

And here is the letter from Mathias Roth, written, as Ludwig von Ficker put it, in 'the orthography of the heart'.

16 Feb. 1914

Dear Herr Ludwig von Ficker!

Excuse me please for only writing you a Card yesterday.

You see at the moment I didnt have any Thing else. To inform you at once that I was leaving for Hall.

Yesterday evening, the 15 Feb I left Innsbruck for Hall. Here I am at the Reserve Hospital School No. 2 in Hall.

May not be here much longer because I will get 2–3 weeks leav then I will go Home.

You will excuse my not writing sooner you see it all came about at the last minute. Would have liked to visit You myself but wasnt allowed out and I was stil very tired. I left to early to Speak to you agin.

You see I always feel so sorry for my Master and I will never forget it all my Life.

And One thing we must never forget is what kind of a Nation we were living among.[63] I am glad that you dear Sir my Master's best colleeg have seen it yourself I wish never to see those pepel agin. And I will never forget You dear Sir ether. I will always always be glad that you visited me in Insbruck too.

If I had known your honorabel name sooner I would have Telegrafed you when he didnt Wake up.

For all my life that will be how I remember those pepel.

I always always think of my Honorabel dear good Master that he had to die such a retched death that way!

Well the evening of the 3rd he was so kind and brotherly and said to me at half past 6 bring me a black coffee next Morning at 7.30 and I should go to Sleep. And on the 4th it came different my dear master didnt need a black coffee any more because the Good Lord had sumoned him in the Night.[64] Yours in Mourning the servant of my loving Master Mathias Roth.

Best regards to you and his family.[65]

The miner Mathias Roth was the only one who followed Trakl's coffin.

The official cause of death was given as cardiac paralysis; in the hospital's records the doctor puts it more precisely: 'Suicide by cocaine intoxication!'—The anamnesis begins as follows: 'Since departing from Innsbruck on 26/VIII Trakl has alternated between states of arousal and catatonia. On the day of the battle of Grodek (14/X) he insisted on going into the front and had to be disarmed by 6 men.—At each base he sought to be transferred into the front as an infantrymen.—Incidentally, in civilian life, rather than practicing his profession, he writes "poetry".'

The word 'poetry' is actually put in quotation marks: true to form.

Did the reader appreciate the '*in*' in the anamnesis—'*in*to the front'—and recall the 'Night Romance': *in the pond—in his cups—in basement vaults—*? No poet could have thought it up.—Karl Röck, in his diary: '10 Nov. Fi sent a card telling of Trakl's death (on 4/5 Nov.). Told this to Luise, she said: "But he was such a fool".'—No more needs to be known about this Luise; she is public opinion.—'Incidentally, in civilian life, rather than practicing his profession, he writes "poetry".'—*All roads end in black putrefaction.*

6.

'And we know his sole, forbidden love to his sister Grete because it is in his poems.'[66]

We admit to racking our brains over these words by Stephan Hermlin: they demand a full unfolding. Of course their author knows perfectly well that a life is one thing and an *oeuvre* another, and that the connection between them is too complex and contradictory to permit direct conclusions. Every autobiography is 'poetry and truth' and as such is not biography, though in a very special sense more authentic than any research findings. And each of a poet's works is a piece of his life; his experience is the substrate of his poetry but not for that reason identical to it. Nothing is more galling, especially in Trakl's case, than an obnoxiously simple-minded equals sign placed between poem and biography, and those who place it act so dreadfully like people in the know.—Trakl's prose poems in particular have thus been pitifully eviscerated: 'as he threw himself before the storming black steeds . . . '; 'as he strangled the cat in the snowy woods . . . ', 'as he—'; enough; it's so arrogantly absurd.—'Dream and Derangement', that most-mined seam, is a poem, not a data set, and the lived reality that went into it is of a material, sensual and mental nature:

living and yearning, fantasy and routine, dreamt derangement, deranged dreaming; the experience of Rimbaud
and the pondering of Kaspar Hauser's fate; and while the
first version is called 'The Downfall of Kaspar Münch'
(with the name *Kermor* also appearing as a variant, a
figure from the fragmentarily preserved play which Trakl
was writing at the same time), this title obscures the fact
that Georg Trakl is describing the downfall of someone
who is a poetic image by Georg Trakl, whose life, then,
does not encompass Trakl's, though Georg Trakl's life
encompasses his. If a poet is a poet indeed, the sum of
his life enters into each poem, but no aspect of this poetic
life must reflect the lived life in the way a protocol reflects
facts.—Lesser than Macbeth, and greater; the witch
describes it perfectly.—Existence in the sphere of the
essential: in this sense, the autobiography of a poet is
more authentic than any biography, even if it is vastly
more poetry than truth. Poetry is 'what remains' and the
poet is the one who creates it.—And so we shall take
Hermlin's statement about Trakl—among the finest
we've read—in the sense that the forbidden love between
brother and sister that is such a peremptory presence in
the poems represents the actual reality, above and
beyond the facts of a biography, the reality of such urgent
concern to readers that they would have to face it even if
the biography spoke against an incestuous relationship.

What is biography allowed to do?

There is an argument, at first quite appealing, that any intrusion into the private sphere of a writer or artist constitutes inadmissible prying; this is true when the intrusion does not rise to its object, that is, when it is in fact prying. The thing intruded on, you see, is no mere privacy, but a privacy in the sphere of posterity, an audience which lends it a different quality: privacy is no longer the purely intimate aspect of a purely individual person, it is the also-public aspect of an exceptional person who, while remaining an individual, has become, through the objective existence of his *oeuvre*, exemplary in a heightened sense, universal in a more concentrated way than a random human life.—The work belongs to the world, and who can separate it from the creator?— This new quality calls for a different protection than that of private rights: each trait in the life of a creator whose work has outlasted his lifetime is now a life-trait of this work, and the biographer must confront it, but will at the same time be measured by it—not by the individual trait as something intimate and private but by the individual trait of a work in the hands of a posterity to whom the biographer conveys the creative life, for that is why he is writing his biography. He always sets himself up against the yardstick of the work and if he does not measure up, he pillories himself as a pryer; yet in the eyes of the public the pillory generally looks like an arch of triumph while it is the life under discussion that seems pilloried. For if every passage into posterity resolves a contradiction of the creator's lifetime—between private life and public work—at the same time it aggravates the contradiction it introduces: between the existence of the work and of what now is a life lived for everyone, and everyone's inability to do justice to it.

During the lifetime of a public figure, he and he alone may determine the extent of his private sphere; let him determine as well how much evidence he chooses to leave of it and the extent of the work he regards as valid (*he*, not his family). Then he may destroy or romanticize, cover his tracks, set traps; but if posterity embraces him, it transforms him so utterly that the most intimate detail of his life, like the worst botch-up in his *oeuvre*, is seen in a public light. Not everything should be published everywhere, but everything should be accessible to everyone: whoever is seized by a poem will want—analogue of understanding—to know all or nothing about the poet; what lies between is a half measure, and that does as little justice to the poet as to the reader who is constantly re-establishing the poem as a poem.—This desire must remain unfulfillable, and that is its contradiction. The singularity of this aesthetic problem has become the tip of a universal one: if humanity is to constitute itself, it must grasp the human being, the person as a whole and the whole person, and 'whole', after all, is not 'half'. And what more compelling object for this grasp, this melting of—as Hans Henny Jahnn states—'the human ice block of lies', than the lives of those who, through the existence of their work, have themselves become a public affair, a *res publica*, more suited than any others to exemplify humanity.

But doesn't this work itself remove them from our daily reality?—So they were long seen and often saw themselves, towering above or sunk fathoms below daily life, made into demigods or vermin by their creativity, and always divorced by their creativity from 'normal' daily routine—how could they be exemplary? But we are convinced that creativity is the property of every person and that its degree, which certainly distinguishes artists from others, is not so much a special dimension that stands out from daily life as an essence that suffuses an existence and heightens all its features: not making an *über-* or an *untermensch*, but making one see more clearly and implacably in this existence the humanity of all. The demonstration of life's unliveability, given by a supreme creative spirit, stands for the daily lives of those who merely suffer, foundering and going under without the God-given ability to speak of it: let them be apprehended through Trakl, through his poem and through his life!

But Trakl didn't fail, did he; didn't Trakl achieve something? Yes: the work of an unliveable life, an objective thing remaining as a symbol of countless purely subjective things of which no trace now tells.—That Trakl's life was unliveable does not lessen his poetry, it defines it more sharply; and that he created a work he sensed would pass into posterity did not make his life liveable;

yet the unity of work and life shatteringly reveals a trait of all humanity.—But aren't the unliveable lives those of an unholy minority; how then could they be exemplary for all? Well, that was Fadeyev's view, thus his blacklists, but even a minority insists on existing, even unliveable lives are human lives, and even when their inability to live becomes such a dominant force that the world calls them neurotics, unliveability is still a trait that distinguishes humans from animals. Perhaps only a potential trait, but we believe that every life contains it, even if its bearer is oblivious or conceals it. If suppressed, it often cracks open like a fissure in the earth—Fadeyev was a severe alcoholic: he drank because he could no longer live life as he'd envisioned it, and at last he reached for the revolver and raised it to his own head: *Cold metal touches my brow / Spiders seek my heart. / There is a light, extinguished in my mouth.*—The shot inscribed him in his own list.—After Yesenin's death Mayakovsky wrote a great poem against suicide, only to shoot himself two years later—who shall cast the first stone at these three? Fadeyev was, and remains, a great writer; it is good to have his work, but shouldn't we know his life as well, doesn't his suicide illuminate Trakl's too and can't Trakl help us grasp something about Fadeyev? *In the evening an icy wind blows from our stars.*—What were the words Becher so liked to cite? 'He who is following a star does not turn back.' A motto of Leonardo da Vinci, harking back to the Bible, to the second chapter of the gospel according to Matthew:

Now when Jesus was born in Bethlehem of Judaea in the days of Herod the king, behold, there came wise men from the east to Jerusalem, saying, Where is he that is born King of the Jews? for we have seen his star in the east, and are come to worship him. When Herod the king had heard these things, he was troubled, and all Jerusalem with him. And when he had gathered all the chief priests and scribes of the people together, he demanded of them where Christ should be born. And they said unto him, In Bethlehem of Judaea [. . .].Then Herod, when he had privily called the wise men, enquired of them diligently what time the star appeared. And he sent them to Bethlehem, and said, Go and search diligently for the young child; and when ye have found him, bring me word again, that I may come and worship him also. When they had heard the king, they departed; and, lo, the star, which they saw in the east, went before them, till it came and stood over where the young child was.

Then came the massacre of the innocents, the dance of death by brown-skinned children.—T. S. Eliot and Rainer Maria Rilke both wrote poems about the three wise men's journey; it is not modernism alone that is one great poem: the poetry and art of all times, taken together, stands as lasting testimony to humanity with all its possibilities and realities.—And testimony must not be mutilated.—In this unholy epoch of an information deluge that floods us with the most trifling things and withholds what is essential, there is a greater need than ever for tidings of human beings, and these tidings turn trifling when manipulated by selection. The essential that is the truth of being is always the whole, which may reveal itself in the part, but a part is an organ of the whole; the torso focuses the form, while a pastiche flattens it and does so precisely when it seems to present a whole.—Thawing, with lies, the human ice block of lies!—They photograph the human face and display its naked features; why do they fear the naked soul?—Ah, they fear they will recognize themselves; they veil the mirror against their own gaze.—'People are not ashamed of thinking something dirty, but are ashamed if they imagine that someone believes them capable of having these dirty thoughts.'[67]—Nietzsche's words hold true. But this 'dirtiness' is also what is human; inhuman are only those paragons of purity from whom the infantilizers of the people have washed all the urine and semen. What is human is the whole human being: in victories and triumphs as in distress and defeat, in temptation and obsession, in splendour and in ordure, in compulsions and in freedom, that in which he is a symbol of dignity and that in which we shudder before him! So intolerable, for this reason, is the insolent claim that only the authorized may learn the whole truth while the multitude of the unauthorized are fed a thin gruel, a digest of life and work: in so doing, those self-appointed authorities prove that they themselves are unauthorized! They claim to fear abuse by the ignorant, but this abuse is unavoidable, as unavoidable as a poem's exposure to misunderstandings, bungling, manias, grotesque misinterpretations, mutilations, distortions, co-option under this banner and that— for example, that of 'authority'. What befalls the work befalls the life as well, and so *schadenfreude* may strut and conceit may preen before it, and so whoever feels the need may gloat over supposedly juicy titbits—he must go to the filthy kitchen to beg for them and will never be asked to the table. You can't protect Velázquez and Giorgione from someone going to bed with the image of their Venus, nor should you sneer at that someone, for his action too is a trait of humanity: no one sniffs at Pygmalion.—They're against abuse and commit it themselves.—They say they're protecting the poet's mystery; but a mystery is always preserved; indeed it becomes the more mysterious the more riddles are solved and shed from it.—They say the masses must be educated; but surely only truth can do that and truth, by nature, is whole.

And so the image of Trakl includes the unspeakable card he saw fit to write to Erhard Buschbeck after visiting a Salzburg brothel in November 1911: *When a Yid fucks, he gets crabs! A Christian hears all the angels singing!* G. T.—It was co-signed by his school and university friend Karl Minnich, of whom no more needs to be known, and

Karl Hauer, ten years older, an outstanding essayist whom Karl Kraus published in *Die Fackel*.—Dirty jokes among the boys? If you will; for us the fitting words are: *Pondering the truth—/ Much pain!*—This fatuous anti-Semitism is a trait of the time; Röck's diaries abound in it, while in Trakl it appears only once, only here, a turbid background setting off that brutally blithe innocence of physical lust that we find over and over again in the Trakl poem: *Rough and brown a moor approaches / Thus to greet you, darling wife.*—*A black horse rears up prodigious; the maid's hyacinth locks / Snatch at the fervour of his purple nostrils.*—*Sublime: to reel drunk through the darkening woods.*—*A Christian hears all the angels singing.*—This innocence in love, wine, drugs and wickedness is the antithesis of crushing guilt in the face of love, wine, drugs and wickedness, often in immediate juxtaposition: *Sublime: to reel drunk through the darkening woods. / Through the black of the branches tormenting bells peal.*—*A tree blazed in red flame; bats flutter up with dark faces.*—*Snow has fallen. After midnight, drunk on purple wine, you leave the dim precinct of people, their hearth's red flame. O the darkness! / Black frost. The ground is hard, the air tastes of bitter things. Your stars align in evil omens.*—*Night menaces the couch of our kisses. / A whisper comes: Who shall relieve you two of guilt?*—For Trakl lust in innocence and guilt in lust are not 'before' and 'after'; they are inextricably interlocked and interpenetrated, one the background of the other, or a black mirror to a white one, physically impossible, but in poetry a magical reality.

And so, by a strange coincidence, an unknown author's parody of Trakl's 'De profundis' has been preserved, it too a companion piece and worth sharing as well; there are things that it reveals. This parody is written on a sheet of paper whose other side Trakl used to draft part of his 'Helian'; it reads:

> There is a whorehouse, where a drunken poet
>   stumbles in
> There is a grey kerbstone, pissed on by dogs
> There is a fart, whose scent wafts past our noses
> What a thing has come to pass.
> At the gate of the house
> The old maidservant collects meagre tips
> Her cloddish eyes greedily pierce the dark of the
>   hall
> The stinking cunt awaits the forceful cock
> In passing
> The watchmen found the drunken corpse
> Puking in the gutter
> And through the alley
> Resounded bawling voices.[68]

Trakl's poem, as understood by one who was assuredly no decadent.—Unliveable life.—The fragment of 'Helian' written on the back, in its final version:

Devastating is the downfall of the race.
At this hour the eyes of the gazer
Fill with the gold of his stars.

A long-silent carillon sinks away at dusk,
The black walls decay on the square,
The dead soldier gives the call to prayer.

A pale angel
The son steps inside his father's empty house.

The sisters have gone abroad to white dotards.
One night the sleeper found them in the hall
   beneath the columns,
Back from unhappy pilgrimages.

O how filth and worms matt their hair
As he steps in with his silver feet
And the others emerge dead from bare rooms.

O you psalms in the fiery rain of midnight
As henchmen smote the gentle eyes with nettles,
And the childish fruits of the elder-bush
Bend wondering over an empty grave.

Yellowed moons roll past softly
Over the youth's fever-linen,
Before the silence of winter comes.

In previous versions the line *The dead soldier gives
the call to prayer* reads: *The guard gives the call to*

prayer—The iron guard gives the call to prayer.—The third to last line once read: *At his head rolls a lonely constellation.*—The line about the *sisters* is seen by most Trakl scholars as referring to Grete's marriage to the much older Arthur Langen.—What does literary historiography know of Georg Trakl's love for Grete Trakl?

The correspondence between Georg and Grete was destroyed by their family. Grete's posthumous papers mysteriously vanished, supposedly stolen from an attic in Berlin. The siblings' closest relatives maintained strict discretion; as for others' testimonials, only a statement by Ludwig von Ficker has survived: 'The prophetic element [. . .] in Trakl comes from this purgatorial fire, the burning bush of his senses in the consciousness of his guilt, perpetrated upon the flesh-and-blood image of his despair. On this matter Trakl was reticence itself, but his sister, who after his death was only a shadow of him- and herself, once confided in me in a fit of desperate self-condemnation; later she took her own life.'[69]—And so, in different ways, poetological or psychoanalytical, scholarship extrapolated from the poem to the life. We shall refrain from judgement; we are relating our experience with Trakl's poetry, which is the mightier reality.

In the mythical landscape of Trakl's poetry his sister is the governing deity—*the sister—the monkess—the youthess—the strangeress*—and in a poem from his early phase, and one of the plays which he destroyed, he names her: *Gret'* and *Grete*.—Scholars have pointed out that from *Night menaces the couch of our kisses. / A whisper comes: Who shall relieve you two of guilt?* and *Siblings in the park glimpse each other trembling* to *The sister's shadow sways through the silent grove / To greet the heroes' spirits, their bleeding heads* the sister's image increasingly shifts towards radiance and sublimity, and they have connected this with Grete's physical distance from Georg. We shall go into the matter only so far as to pose a question of the reader's which we once dimly asked ourselves: Why, if it is not a problem of our own, are we touched so essentially by the carnal love between brother and sister in the Trakl poem?

An explanation is at hand: It brings the poet closer to us as a human being.—Well and good, but in what sense is he brought closer to us?

Or: in what sense do we draw closer to him?

We offer a simple explanation: we believe that the reader who is moved without feeling affected actually is affected by the situation.

In the relationship between brother and sister, the closest and the furthest are yoked together in a contradiction: the most easily attained unattainable.—Little Brother and Little Sister.—

Then the brother said, 'Sister, I am thirsty; if I knew of a little brook I would go and just take a drink; I think I hear one running.' The brother got up and took the little sister by the hand, and they set off to find the brook.

But the wicked stepmother was a witch, and had seen how the two children had gone away, and had crept after them privily, as witches do creep, and had bewitched all the brooks in the forest.

Now when they found a little brook leaping brightly over the stones, the brother was going to drink out of it, but the sister heard how it said as it ran, 'Who drinks of me will be a tiger, who drinks of me will be a tiger.' Then the sister cried, 'Pray, dear brother, do not drink, or you will become a wild beast, and tear me to pieces.' The brother did not drink, although he was so thirsty, but said, 'I will wait for the next spring.'

When they came to the next brook the sister heard this also say, 'Who drinks of me will be a wolf, who drinks of me will be a wolf.' Then the sister cried out, 'Pray, dear brother, do not drink, or you will become a wolf, and devour me.' The brother did not drink, and said, 'I will wait until we come to the next spring, but then I must drink, say what you like; for my thirst is too great.'

And when they came to the third brook the sister heard how it said as it ran, 'Who drinks of me will be a roebuck; who drinks of me will be a roebuck.' The sister said, 'Oh, I pray you, dear brother, do not drink, or you will become a roe-buck, and run away from me.' But the brother had knelt down at once by the brook, and had bent down and drunk some of the water, and as soon as the first drops touched his lips he lay there a young roebuck.[70]

A young roebuck, doubly harmless: a non-predator and a non-adult; it'll do its little sister no harm. The contradiction is eliminated—but don't we feel it still in the tiger and the wolf? *Beneath dark firs / Two wolves mingled their blood / In a stony embrace.*—The poem containing these lines is called 'Passion'.—Walther Killy points out the connection between the adjective 'stony' and the myth of the Propoetides which Ovid mentions in the tenth book of his *Metamorphoses*: Cypriot maidens who denied Aphrodite's divinity, at which the goddess of love drove them to give themselves indiscriminately to every comer; awakening from their delusion, they turned to stone.—And did we note the sister's fear that the roebuck might flee her?—You believe you can conquer sex, then it conquers you and you are petrified by guilt.—In one of his last poems Trakl points back to the origin: *The Titans' dark sagas.*—A few lines before that he writes: *Sister, your two brows of blue / Beckon silent in the night.*

These dark sagas are sagas of incest, incest over three generations: the Titans, rulers of the universe, are sons and daughters of Mother Earth and Father Heaven, who himself is the son of Mother Earth. The twice seven Titans, brothers and sisters, live coupled together as one flesh, and of the children that proceed from the most august of these marriages, that of Kronos and Rhea, two again, and again the noblest, shall be man and wife as brother and sister, and their names are Zeus and Hera.— For the very next generation, Apollo and Artemis, the twins, such a relationship would be an inconceivable sacrilege, or—speaking with Plato's severity—'hateful to the gods and the most shameful of shameful things'.[71]

Incest became taboo.

We can call on these dark sagas to illuminate many a line of this poem, sagas not only of incest but also of every hateful thing conceivable: the castration of the father, the expulsion of the mother, the devouring of the children, the war of the begotten against their begetter, poison and sickle, rape and dethronement and the unleashing of all the monsters that the deepest darkness holds.—*Red the ore resounds in shafts*—what resounds beneath that? *Mother must fear for her child*—so did Rhea fear for her children, devoured by her husband Kronos, and Grete awaited her abortion.—*Lust, tears, stony pain*—it is a progression throughout the eons and a formula of each moment.

It is a dark saga that Trakl tells, speaking back in time, to an origin in innocence: *Beneath dark firs / Two wolves mingled their blood / In a stony embrace; golden / The cloud dissolved over the jetty, / Patience and silence of childhood.*—Ah, Little Brother, Little Sister: when the flesh awakens, what is closest to each is the other, yet the other is furthest of all: the most forbidden thing.—Just stretch out your hand: the forbidden fruit.—'"Sister, I am thirsty; if I knew of a little brook I would go and just take a drink; I think I hear one running."—"Pray, dear brother, do not drink, or you will become a wild beast, and tear me to pieces."'—You have forgotten.—In the fairy tale Little Brother becomes a young roebuck that can do Little Sister no harm and Little Sister remains in the human realm, though suffocated by the hellfire the wicked stepmother prepares in her bath. Yet the Grimms relate another version that has come down to us as a song, and it is usually with this plot that the tale circulates among other peoples, the Hungarians, for example, or the Turks: here Little Brother as a roebuck is being chased by the stepmother's bloodhounds, and in his dire need calls up to Little Sister's window:

> Ah, little sister, save me!
> The dogs of the lord they chase me;
> They chase me, oh! so quickly;
> They seek, they seek to rend me,
> They wish to drive me to the arrows,
> And thus to rob me of my life.

But Little Sister has also been transformed into a beast, a duck, and she laments in reply:

> Patience, dear brother mine,
> I lie in the lowest depths,
> The earth is the bed I sleep on,

The water it is my coverlid,
Patience, dear brother mine,
I lie in the lowest depths.[72]

Both are beasts, their innocence lost, but in a fairy tale still and so they are saved. In the fairy tale they are always Little Brother and Little Sister; in life they are brother and sister and it is a fairy tale no longer. The brother cries from the depths to his sister: *De profundis clamavi ad te*! and the sister cried likewise to her brother, but all we hear now is the brother's voice; the sister's voice was music, and what she wrote has been lost.—In fairy tales all reality lives on, albeit fragmented and frozen, and in the Trakl poem the fairy tales come to life: *You dream: the sister combs her blonde hair*—no doubt it was once golden.—*A golden ray breaks through the roof and spills down / Upon the siblings dreamy and confused* —the glimmer-rain in Danae's lap.—*Sister, when I found you by a lonely glade / In the woods, at noon, and the animal's silence was vast.*—*The sister's pale form stepped from putrefying blue and thus spake her bleeding mouth: Prick black thorn.* [. . .] *and softly from the sister's silver wound ran blood and fell on me a fiery rain.*

These are fairy tales no longer.

The contradiction of brother and sister—that they are man and woman and not man and wife—contains all that is uncovetable and coveted and all that is unconsciously coveted and all lies open and shut away, how could it not touch us? It is the contradiction of the taboo:

what is so possible and yet so impossible, the humanly normal social abnormity and the socially normal human abnormity, without any middle ground: a taboo works on a profoundly existential level, or not at all.—There are societies that do not shun incest, indeed that cultivate it, like the Incas, just as there are societies in which cannibalism is a communal activity while most regard it as abhorrent.[73] Neither, in itself, goes against humanity; a taboo is not an inhuman thing that is proscribed, but a human thing made inhuman. For a brother to sleep with his sister, for a clan to eat the corpse of the deceased at a ceremonial meal, is either routine or monstrous. And so the bursting of the taboo-contradiction happens either on the highest or the lowest moral level (always assuming, of course, that the taboo is recognized as a taboo): the drunken beast of a father who habitually preys upon his daughter without 'thinking much of it', without feeling more than a dim sense of wrong; or the violation—highly conscious, defiantly rebellious and yet utterly innocent, yearning for salvation—of a commandment felt to be contrary to nature, and from and in this violation the most profound sense of guilt. This highly conscious *acting nonetheless* is kin to blasphemy, the conscious desecration of what is held holy, which, after all, is only blasphemy when holiness is believed in. The unbeliever does not act blasphemously, his actions are merely condemned as such by the pious; no guilt oppresses him, yet he also lacks what the blasphemist actually desires: the lust for that which makes him guilty, the lust for rebellion against the order which he simultaneously recognizes.

In this sense Trakl's poems are deeply blasphemous and deeply tormented by blasphemy: incest wrecks him, yet he is not afraid to address a cycle of the most heartfelt and (for that very reason) most iniquitous poems to his sister as *Rosary Songs*: *At night stars seek, Good Friday child, / The vault that is your brow.*—To a pious person that must seem monstrous, and Trakl is a pious Christian. The star that leaves its orbit in haste to do homage is the Star of Bethlehem; the child of Good Friday, the day of Christ's death, is the anti-Christ-ess and the night is of that midnight towards which the blind clock-hands climb.—*O the nearness of death. Let us pray. / In this night on tepid cushions / Incense-yellowed, the lovers' slender limbs fall slack.*—A black Mass; blasphemy.—And deepest, purest innocence, capable of using nymph and monkess on equal footing in different versions: *Monkess, close me in your darkness, / Cross in cool stars a-sparkle. / Purple crack of lips and lies / Death throes of a bell on high. / Night your lustful cloudy dark- ness / Scarlet fruit, infernal lies / Death throes of a bell on high—/ Bleeding cross in stars a-sparkle.*—This is the third version of a poem, 'Ode to the Night', which would ultimately be called 'Night Surrender'.—The *monkess* is not a nun, who would be the monk's spiritual sister, his sister in Christ; the *monkess* is the Other to the monk *and* the nun, and the brother of the monkess would be

the he-nun, not a brother in Christ but in Satan.—
Blasphemy engendered!—Baudelaire conjured the contradiction of I and anti-I to its extreme, unto death: 'I am
the wound, and yet the blade! / The slap, and yet the
cheek that takes it! / The limb, and yet the wheel that
breaks it, / The torturer, and he who's flayed!'[74]—
Formula of the unliveable life that each of us must live.

In his work *Sex and Character*—hotly debated at the
time, now quite unjustly forgotten—Otto Weininger, a
contemporary of Trakl's who died young by his own
hand, described the contradictory essence of each human
being as a melding of woman and man or man and
woman, his formula being that a man instinctively seeks
the woman whose male share, together with his, yields a
whole man, just as the female share in her partner com-
pletes her to become a whole woman.—And it is
Weininger who said: 'Ultimately . . . understanding a
person means having him and his opposite in oneself.'[75]
—This could be extended to the poem as well. Every
person as a hermaphrodite, as a communion of man-part
and woman-part, in each fibre, in each cell, in each
thought, in each action—from Karl Röck's diaries we
know the fascination of these thoughts and the urgency
with which they were discussed, by Trakl as well.

This hermaphrodism is a trait of Trakl's poetry; the
reader will have noticed his predilection for the neuter,
for nominalized adjectives in which male and female
merge to a neuter in the linguistic sense as well: instead of

a masculine or feminine word for 'blossom' we have 'a blossoming thing' ['*ein Blühendes*'].—Just as, according to Weininger, the man-part and woman-part of both partners do not unite to form a whole man and a whole woman until they achieve the state of being man-and-woman, precisely because they are now *one* flesh, so too does Trakl's poetry seek neologisms for this yearned-for completion: *monkess—youthess—strangeress.*—In the fourth version of 'Ode to the Night', the *monkess* becomes a *nymph*, a consort of Pan and the fauns who surrenders herself with abandon; this strengthens the erotic element in one direction but flattens it all around: *Nymph, draw me into your darkness; / Aster shivers by the path / Sadness blooms in women's laps, / Bleeding cross in stars a-sparkle. // Purple crack of lips and lies / In a cool mouldering chamber; / Laughs and golden games are still heard; / Death throes of a bell on high. // Cloud of blue! Black from the tree / Falls the fruit too spoilt to save / And the room becomes a grave / And life's dim toil becomes a dream.*—The bleeding cross is the cross of Good Friday: 'The Jews therefore, because it was the preparation, that the bodies should not remain upon the cross on the Sabbath day, (for that Sabbath day was an high day), besought Pilate that their legs might be broken, and that they might be taken away. Then came the soldiers, and brake the legs of the first, and of the other which was crucified with him. But when they came to Jesus, and saw that he was dead already, they brake not his legs: But one of the soldiers with a spear pierced his side, and forthwith came there out blood and water' (John 19: 31 34).—The fifth version, 'Night Surrender', published in *Der Brenner*, invokes the monkess once again, and indeed the nymphs and fauns of the early poems are altogether absent from the late work; Endymion, Aphrodite and Helios vanish too, but Cyclops and the Titans and Orpheus appear instead, at first alongside Christ, no: *Kristus*, and then without this name and nonetheless with it, invoking in monstrous blasphemy and heartfelt devotion the birth of what both saves and damns:

> When Orpheus' silver touch stirs the lyre,
> Mourning a dead thing in the evening garden,
> Who are you that rest under tall trees?
> The murmur of lament, the autumn trees,
> The blue pond,
> Expiring beneath budding trees
> And following the sister's shadow;
> Dark love
> Of an unruly race
> That day flees on golden wheels.
> Silent night.

—The beginning of Trakl's 'Passion'.

We feel we have done justice to those words: ' . . .we know his sole, forbidden love to his sister Grete because it is in his poems'.—The *monkess* first appears in the first version of that cycle of poems devoted to the *Night*; entitled 'In the Snow', it reads: *Pondering the truth— /*

Much pain! / *At last inspiration* / *Unto death*. / *Winter night* / *You immaculate monkess*!

It is the sheer innocence of guilt unto death.

In the night that revealed Trakl's life to me, I saw my father again and again; I saw him in the photo of the moustachioed one-year volunteer Georg Trakl as though it were his portrait, and I saw him, again and again, in that terrifying image from 1909 or 1910 known as the 'picture in the oval frame': in an oval cut from a grey rectangle, the left (from the viewer's perspective: the right) half of the face shadowed almost past recognition, bare from the hair parting to below the collarbone, unabashedly brutal, staring in the intoxication of ether, excruciating self-exposure, the mien of a man who has murdered himself.—I saw my father, younger by twenty years, overwhelmed by alcohol, speech slurred, climbing the stairs from his vault, only that he lacked the strain of truthfulness that makes this photo so harrowing: thus did the Baroque depict human beings, half flesh brimming with sensuality, half corruption.

That night, faced with that photo, however foolish it may sound, I suddenly felt—well, what?—a sort of duty on the part of posterity to make mental amends for society's sins against Trakl; in all respects I saw him as a victim.—It was the time when Franz Kafka's work became available here at last, after long, incomprehensible prohibitions; wasn't it time to make Trakl's work known as well? I argued the case, sometimes speaking of my parting conversation with my father, and so it happened that the publisher Philipp Reclam jun. asked me to make a selection of his poems for a volume in their *Universalbibliothek*. My editorial duties would have included an afterword, but quite rightly I felt unequal to writing an essay at the time (in the end the book appeared much later, I believe four or five years after the manuscript was delivered), so the publisher commissioned Stephan Hermlin. To this day I am grateful to the instinct that kept from doing my duty. Setting aside the stylistic issues, I would surely have done what now seems the worst possible transgression—I would have commended Trakl's life to the reader's forbearance and tried to bring his work into a line leading to socialist literature, not in the sense of that one great poem in which the poetry of all ages and languages converges (and so, too, that of a socialist stance or confession), nor in the sense of one of those harbingers that like sudden bird flights or fires in the sky presage a great convulsion, but very much in the sense of the word 'line' as a one-dimensional connection: *actually* socialist realism, only—excusably so—not yet conscious of the fact and thus excusably imperfect.—The selection of poems would then have had to prove what I alleged of the *oeuvre*.

I vividly recall how hard it was to give up the afterword, as I was already working out bits of the biography, such as the love between Georg and Grete—I saw it as a moral defect but one to be blamed less on the siblings

than on their society. So, too, Trakl's drug addiction; so
too his professional travails; so too his melancholy. In a
nutshell: what I utterly failed to grasp was that Trakl's
life was the price he had to pay to accomplish his work
in the way he did accomplish it: as the testimony of an
unliveable life. At the time I was far removed from the
insight that dawned on me only with E. T. A. Hoffmann:
an artist is one who can do no other—and who then
cannot be helped.—By seeking to separate Trakl's life
from his work, I showed that I was more remote from
both than ever before; it was very strange, but so it was—
at the very moment I took a stand for Trakl, I did it in
the way that makes the beneficiary groan: Lord, save me
from my friends!—I sought excuses everywhere, aimed
to smooth over, to downplay, to put right in the sense of
unambiguous rightness; it was a bad business. Essentially,
it came down to proving that this decadence wasn't decadence at all. At the time I was quite preoccupied with
'Grodek'; I vividly recall how I thought to resolve *All
roads end in black putrefaction* into the landscape.—
Now, those roads are surely landscape as well, even originally landscape, those roads that peter out into the mud,
the mud of the vastness of black earth, the mud of the
war-ravaged East, but they are also roads of the soul and
also roads of society, and that 'also' was something I
failed to grasp.

The desire to understand the Trakl poem manifested
itself as the delusion that I could conclusively define it: I

know I pondered for days and days in the attempt to pin down that *Under vaults of thorns*: botanical or architectural vaults? I grasped only an exclusive 'or'; his 'both this and this'[76] escaped me. Yet assistance came from Trakl himself: his 'or', which surprises us in 'Psalm', is just another aspect of the 'also': unfolding, but admittedly separation as well. In this period Trakl's figures fled me to escape petrifaction as fixed terms; I no longer saw his angel and I dared not think of *Helian* or *Elis*—to whom could I have pinned them?—yet I was profoundly convinced that this unambiguous fixation existed. But even as Trakl's myths fled me, I was spellbound by the images of reality I beheld over and over in his biography: the house of his birth, his garden, his streets and churches, his pharmacy, his brothel, his pubs, his mountains and his sky, his handwriting, his manuscripts and again and again that face staring out from the oval frame.—Was *he* the madman of his 'Psalm'?—I resisted the thought, then recalled that there had been several madmen in the House of Habsburg and a suicide tragedy exactly at Trakl's time, love and death in romantic landscapes, could that be the clue? I studied pre-war Austrian history, immersed myself in biographies of archdukes, sought enlightenment in the polemics of Karl Kraus, but the more I read my way around Trakl, the more his poem faded.

Only when I gave up the thought of an afterword and focused solely on selecting the poems, not so much for the publication's sake as to reclaim Trakl for myself, did it re-emerge, now overwhelming, in its form of flames, as a rain of fire; it was like a poetic Pentecost. Only then, in total surrender, when I no longer read to understand as I had hitherto understood understanding, that is, as a conveyance towards something pre-fixed which the poem was only supposed to confirm—only when I read with no condition but to have Trakl for myself did I understand him, experiencing him anew. I had read him thus before, as the night bent its broken brow over me and my father; now I read once again with the frisson of grasping what was my own affair, the frisson of experience: *tua res agitur.*—It was an understanding in the Pentecostal sense: 'And how hear we every man in our own tongue, wherein we were born?'—A rupture: something new began.—All at once I understood Trakl's language; all at once I understood Trakl's images; and all at once I ceased to understand the man I was just now: twilight and decay; what had decayed, which light was waning and which light was waxing?

I believe that the selection I made then, in the course of one night, stands up even today; I remember that I did hesitate to include 'The Young Maid' or 'Night Romance', which seemed too crassly decadent; that word still had the force of taboo. That night, in a Leipzig hotel where I'd taken Trakl's poems along on a trip (whose reason I have long since forgotten) I saw once more the image of my teacher, and I heard his '*tertium non datur*', but it had turned against him.—I agreed with him: Wholly, or not at all. And even a part, as a selection, was not a third thing; either a part that stood for the whole, or a part that traduced the whole, that is, a sham, and thus not even a part any more.—I included the two poems, and if I had hesitated at first, now I was all the more voracious.

This decision concluded a battle that doctrine and poetry had waged within me for more than twenty years; I did not grasp this outcome at the time, though it was the door to understanding, and only today do I know what then I barely sensed, expressed in that voracity: Trakl's poem had prevailed.

7.

I am not writing an autobiography; I am telling of my experiences with the Trakl poem, but they are part of my biography and this part appears here as a whole, so I must confront the reader's question: was Trakl responsible for my development? One verse, and a life leaves its orbit, leaping to a different, opposed track?—Sigh . . .— Developments are unrepeatable and once they've happened as they happened, a 'what if?' seems pointless; but the question has already been posed.—'It's just incredible how this Trakl has seduced you,' one reader of the manuscript moaned, and he pictured the consequences.

And has it not been conceded that poetry works like fate?

I shall take the reader's question and try, by two different routes, to arrive at an answer. First: what in my life would be different, what would have happened differently, if I had not encountered Trakl, if in that antiquarian bookshop in Karlsbad I hadn't come across the large-format volume with pale-blue titles over the blocks of verse?

I would have walked into my parental home as I did and I'd have left it as I did with my marching orders to

Dresden—without the shock of my heart's lake filling with chalk and an icy wind blowing down from the stars of our victories, but five days later I'd have had to grasp that the war was lost, and the poetic beacon of this realization would no doubt have been Rilke's verses, 'The Stylite', perhaps, which I still know by heart and in which I now detect a strange kinship with Trakl's 'Downfall': 'Surmising *he* was lost, he looked aloft. / Escaping from the peoples' stench, he rose / with clawing hands: he climbed a pillar's shaft // that seemed to rise for ever, till it soared / no more.'[77]—this too a climbing towards midnight, and the worms that dripped from the angel's lids would have fallen from the wounds of the hermit howling above the world's doings. His lamentations would have been mine, his howling my howling, his wailing my wailing: 'But now my tree of jubilation breaks, / My slow jubilation tree / breaks in the storm. / Loveliest thing in my invisible / landscape, you that made me more easily seen / by angels, themselves invisible.'[78]—The angel again.—'Yet his face, as with dial-hands coinciding, / reads midnight'[79]—this is said of a magician.—Is he playing with white serpents? The kinship alarms me. But, after all, they are poems of the same era and both poets are Austrians.

Rilke then, not Trakl; perhaps Stefan George, too; probably Weinheber no longer; and he would have lain beside me on the ship that took us to Novorossiysk; and the worker in the tangle of iron would have smacked his fist over his thumb in just the same way, under Stalin's smile, above the water with its iridescent slick; and the rubble of the city; and the march into the mountains; and then I'd have hunkered on my cot and scratched poems on a shingle, wretched laments of the wretched hangover after the intoxication of ruling the world, yet even so self-knowledge would have stirred, and the quiet work of the burnt vineyard and the murdered orphans would have been done by Rilke's beggars and prisoners and lepers: all poetry works as *one* great poem.—That I was sent to the anti-fascist school had nothing to do with Trakl, and the doctrinal conflict would have been sparked by another banned poet's work—probably Rilke, perhaps Benn, but perhaps Trakl after all; it is inconceivable that the Trakl poem would never have entered my life, and at the very latest my endeavours in Czech poetry, for example, my familiarity with František Hrubín, who subtitled one of his poems 'While Reading Georg Trakl', would have brought me to the 'Psalm'.—Admittedly without the conversation in my parental home, and I would not have experienced to the same degree the rending imperative to reject as the quintessence of perdition what seemed like salvation; but today I venture to say that the intuition of plunging into national catastrophe would have found some other way to enter my awareness lightning-like in verse form. After all, this plunge was heralded by the poems I myself wrote manically every night of the war: scorched lands, scorched seas, stars smashing down, icy storms, the Vandals' downfall in the desert, Odysseus' sinking crew, the fall of the Nibelungs beyond the shattered bridge—wouldn't these erratic, dilettantish efforts have sought at last a valid yardstick? It may seem mystical to some, but I believe in poetry, for it works like fate—provided you stand within its magic circle. Those outside will never feel its power. Those inside feel it fully, and it governs their whole life.

The conflict between poetry and doctrine was inevitable; both were rooted within me and both, for me, were existential. I was serious about doctrine, behind which, however twisted the features, I still saw the face of the liberators of Auschwitz, and I was serious about poetry, in which I saw the Other that even after Auschwitz refused to give up on humanity, for that Other is always the Other to Auschwitz.—One seriousness balanced the other.—There can be no talk of 'seduction' here; this word belittles not only poetry but doctrine—that is to say, belittles what is behind it. My conflict erupted from within, not from without, so it was not avoidable. No end to it is yet in sight.

I plan to describe this experience—which, as I begin to grasp, has governed my life ever since childhood—as precisely and comprehensively as possible, in all its many-stranded intertwinement with daily life and world affairs, which are mirrors of one another. And so I would rather not anticipate details; but the reader's question begs an example, and I shall hint at one.

The events of summer 1968 caused,[80] in my development, one of those ruptures in which the unity of the personality asserts itself as discontinuity—what might they and their consequences have to do with the work of Georg Trakl? Nothing at all, in the sense that those events would have happened just as they happened independent of the work of any poet—yet everything, in the sense that the conflict embodied on a world-historical scale the contradiction that I had experienced within myself, that had strained me to the breaking point and that would not have been thinkable without Trakl. To the breaking point: I confess that during those days a black road opened up before me; in the end, I chose the road of bright consciousness and found the strength to break with the white magician, the sweet drug of distilled grain to whose spell, year after year, I had consciously resorted more and more. This decision too was independent of Trakl, yet bound with him in every fibre: he was in my life wholly and thus wholly in the decision that changed my life from the ground up, even to my external appearance. —Ah, it is an awkward business, always having to prove anew that a life is the life that it is.—But I will say this much: in a dream I dreamt in the drying-out centre at the psychiatric clinic in Rostock, I was carousing with my father and Georg Trakl was watching, bending forward, a bobble hat on his head and a child's rattle in his hand. I argued angrily with my father; he watched without saying a word or shaking the rattle; he stood smiling like death, an awkward smile, and suddenly he vanished and our argument ended as well and we melted away into crumbling rubble.—I understand this dream; I could even explain it.—I recall still other dreams with Trakl, but I will share no more of them.

This is the first road towards an answer: even if I try to imagine my life without the chance antiquarian purchase, from a certain point onward it would have unfolded essentially as it did. The second road would be to consider whether some turning point in my life might have led me in a completely different direction even after encountering Trakl in May 1945, and here I nod as I write. When I realized that the war was lost, I wanted to join the Foreign Legion or, rather, any foreign legion.—I hoped that the English still possessed such an institution; the French legion seemed likely to involve too many chicaneries, but the English legion seemed acceptable. I was twenty-three, with my A levels and knowledge of no profession but that of the soldier; I could operate a machine gun, a grenade launcher and various signalling devices; I could lay cables, set up pylons and climb them with climbing irons; I was still hobbling on a stick, but even on a stick I'd marched a whole day long through Bohemia's forests, so why not through a Malaysian jungle?—Like tens of thousands of others, I was trying to evade the Red Army: the Americans had reached the Elbe, beyond which we believed freedom lay; for me its name was 'the Foreign Legion'. On my last postcard from the front (it never reached its addressees), I hinted at this

decision to my parents; I did not succeed in realizing it.—
What happened, happened.—My father resorted to the
vial of poison; my mother and sister were packed off into
a freight car and trundled off into the burnt Reich; I
was taken prisoner by the Soviets and sailed to
Novorossiysk.—I can easily picture my life's course if my
escape plan had succeeded: missing in action at Algiers
or Dien Bien Phu. Nothing would have dissuaded me
from my plan; Trakl would have gone with me, across
the vineyard with holes full of spiders, and the poems I'd
surely have scribbled night after night on scraps of paper
would not have differed from those I wrote in Hitler's
army, except that an angel would have dwelt there,
worms dripping from his lids, with faeces-stained wings.
Yet perhaps a flyer with poems by Eluard or Ho Chi
Minh would have fallen into my hands, or a brochure by
Sartre, or an essay by Camus, or the news of Auschwitz
would have sufficed. But instead of losing myself in What
Ifs, I wish to call to mind a poem, one that must enter
the calculation whenever you speak of existence; it is a
valid variable not to be ignored. It grew dear to me by
way of Trakl, pondering his truth—Goethe's 'Primal
Words, Orphic':[81]

ΔAIMΩN, *Daimon*

When you were granted here your brief
   admission,
As sun and planets met that day they charted
For evermore your growing to fruition

According to the law by which you started.
Thus must you be, from self there's no remission,
Thus long have sibyls, prophets this imparted;
Nor any time nor any power can shatter
Imprinted form informing living matter.

TYXH, *Chance*

But easing change gets round that stern
    constriction
As with and round us change is all-imbuing;
No more alone, you grow through social friction
And do such deeds as any man is doing.
This life's an ebb and flow, a contradiction,
A toy that's played with, play for our pursuing.
The years have quietly formed the circle's
    essence,
The lamp awaits the flame of incandescence.

EPΩΣ, *Love*

And come it must!—He plunges earthwards
    winging
Who from the timeless void to heaven once sped,
On airy pinions hovering and swinging
All springtime's day around the heart and head,
Away and back again for ever springing,
Then woe is weal, there's sweet delights in dread.
So many soaring hearts are dissipated,
The noblest to the One is dedicated.

ΑΝΑΓΚΗ, *Necessity*

Then back once more, to what the stars had
  fated:
Conditioning and law; and wish from willing
Can only come since we are obligated,
Our will then all our fitful fancies killing;
Its dearest from the heart is extirpated,
Hard 'Must' prevails, both will and fancy
  stilling.
Thus, though we seem free, yet constrictions
  bind us
More closely still than those that first confined
  us.

ΕΛΠΙΣ, *Hope*

But such a confine, such a wall immuring
In odious chafe, is breached and left ungated
Though like the timeless crags it seem enduring!
A Being rises light and liberated:
Through showering rain and cloud and mist
  obscuring
She lifts us up, we soar on wings elated:
You know her well, ranging all zones to find us;
One wingbeat—and the aeons lie behind us!

8.

All roads end in black putrefaction—'Where else?', we are tempted to ask. If you embrace the concept of becoming, the idea of perpetual emergence and fading, birth and deathbed, blossoming and decaying, that 'all that comes to be deserves to perish wretchedly', you must learn to endure finding yourself on a road that will one day arrive in putrefaction; the question is what begins beyond that.—What follows the midnight to which the blind clock-hands climb? 'Pure nothing, it is all the same'?—In 'Last Night', the epilogue of *The Last Days of Mankind*, Karl Kraus evoked this planet's obliteration, a chronicle in stage directions: 'Raging of flames'—'Thunder of worlds'—'Downfall'—'Hush'—'Vast silence'; in between are the choruses of the jingoistic optimists.—The prophet was reproached for the awkward fact of composing an apocalypse that he himself survived; the same accusation could be levelled at Trakl, but in both cases it would miss the point. That Last Night, that Midnight is yet to come; only its form has been summoned or, rather, aspects of its form which the Evangelist voiced: 'I must work the works of him that sent me, while it is day: the night cometh, when no man can work' (John 9:4).

Grodek

At dusk the autumn woods resound
With deadly weapons, the golden plains
And blue lakes, above them the sun
More darkly rolling; the night enfolds
Dying warriors, the wild lament
Of their broken mouths.
But silent in the willow vale—
Red clouds in which a wrathful god dwells—
The spilt blood gathers, moonlike coolness;
All roads end in black putrefaction.
Beneath the gold boughs of the night and the
stars
The sister's shadow sways through the silent
grove
To greet the heroes' spirits, their bleeding heads;
And the dark flutes of autumn resound softly in
the reeds.
O prouder grief! you iron altars
Today the spirit's hot flame is fed by a vast pain,
The grandchildren unborn.

All roads end in black putrefaction—the most terrible of these words is 'all' (as the most terrible of John's words are 'no man'), and the question is how to take it: as diachrony or synchrony.

In a diachronic sense, this line—inadmissibly reduced to its philosophical content—would mean nothing but the law of becoming: every road shall one day lead to putrefaction. Taken synchronically, it is devastating: today, whichever road you take, all end, within sight, in the same moorland; and you cry out, for so many countries are yet untravelled, so many works are yet undone. This 'all' speaks of a world without alternatives, end times; all history has become meaningless—but did it become so, or was it always meaningless? Certainly it has been so, but did it have to become so, was its becoming always without alternative, was *this* end already contained in its beginning such that no other end could follow? Not just any end: this end-too-soon?—The reader baulks at such questions: was Trakl writing philosophy of history? Wasn't he speaking of his moment, his life-long death-hour, which in every human life is the moment without alternatives? To be sure, 'Grodek' speaks of this moment; but we feel affected.—The questions do not spring from Trakl's poem, though we pose them from its vantage point. This line stands as the poem's centre: What goes before it? And what follows it?

What goes before it is the battle; what goes before that is the landscape.

A lovely landscape: autumnal woods, a golden plain, blue lakes, a rolling sun, but it is a loveliness under threat; the deadly weapons still resound in it and the rolling sun was always dark here, as the comparative form 'more darkly' shows. The battle has only made it still darker, this battle is an outcome, not an incursion—

it was inherent in the landscape.—Landscape means the human world, not nature alone; or nature broken by humans.—It is the landscape reaching unto death, the landscape of the evening, the setting sun, the Occident, which Trakl's late work invokes again and again: *Moon, like a dead thing / Stepping from a blue cave, / And many blossoms fall / Upon the rocky path*—thus begins his poem 'Occident' and thus it ends: *You great cities / Erected stony / On the plain! / How mutely / The exile / With his dark brow follows / The wind, the hill's bare trees. / You rivers that glimmer from afar! / Great is the alarm / Of evening's awful glow / In the storm clouds. / You dying peoples! / Pale wave / Shattering on night's shore, / Falling stars.*—It is the landscape of Hölderlin that erupts in these late poems, and behind it lies Greece.

Silence likes to dwell in Trakl's poems, but here in 'Grodek' it has fled and what remains is a monstrous muteness; even the mortally wounded warriors do not cry out, no lament issues from their broken mouths, they *are* the lament: mouthless mouth—Laocoön. And just beyond Grodek is Troy; Trakl's poem affects us in part because it speaks of Now with the words of the Old, the words most densely freighted. *Warriors* and *weapons*, not 'gunners' and 'shells', and *stony city* speaks of Thebes as well as Vienna. The muteness of the landscape is silence no longer; something else has moved into silence's dwelling-place: *But silent in the willow vale— / Red clouds in which a wrathful god dwells— / The spilt blood* gathers, *moonlike coolness*; / *All roads end in black putrefaction.*—Will the god outlast this putrefaction?— All hope seems to rest in the word *dwells*, but how long has wrath dwelt among the peoples, and when a god is wroth, won't he smite humankind once again? Or is his wrath itself putrefaction? Trakl's poem gives no answer; *wrath* is a new word for him, only in the war does it grow more familiar: *The dark wrath of the people / Is like the winter storm's wild organ music*—the first draft has 'the old ones' instead of *the people.*—It appeared only once before: *Raging, God's wrath lashes the brows of the obsessed*; and the name of that poem is 'To Those Now Silent'.

It is strange and at the same time it is not: in this poetic *oeuvre* which is tuned so fully to the vowel O, in which the rhyming words *Dorn* and *Korn* appear over and over, and *Brot* and *rot* and *Odem* and *wohnen* and *Tod*; *Gold*; *Schoss*; *Rohr*; *Mord*; *Mond*; *Mohn*; *Moos*; *Rost*; *Stroh*; *Strom*; *Frost*; *Wolf*; *Dorf*; *Kost*; *Korb*; *Gott*; *Drossel*; *Glocke*; *Sonne*; and *Dornenbogen* and *rosig* and *Woge*,[82] and the pure vowel O, which stands for every emotion, *Wort* with the plural *Worte*, and the conjugated verbs: *tropft*; *schmolz*; *bog*; *log*; *gestorben*; *zerbrochen*[83]—in this *oeuvre*, before August 1914, the word *Zorn*, wrath, appears but that one time, it is reserved for God, and 'wrathful' appears only once as well: *White high priest of truth, / Crystal voice in which God's icy breath dwells, / Wrathful magician, / Beneath whose flaming mantle the warrior's blue armour rings.*—This quatrain captures the figure of Karl Kraus.—As Trakl could not know, and yet knew, one of the wrathful who dwelt in the red clouds where the spilt blood gathered was Kraus, with the thunder of the word and the lightning of scorn, and he lent to the mouths of the mute that language which the wrathless was unable to give them: 'Curse you, Kaiser! I feel your hand, / Full of poison and night and fatherland! / It smells of pestilence, the death of hope. / Your gaze is the gallows, your beard the rope!'—And the gallows of the trees outside that barn and the ninety wounded men before whom Trakl experienced his most terrible helplessness; Karl Kraus made them speak as well:

> Come faster—come faster—
> I'm stretched—on—the—rack here—
> a plaster, Herr Doktor,
> is all that I'm after!
>
> For hours I've swooned—
> with so many wounds—
> they're bleeding, they're bleeding—
> no plaster to soothe.
>
> My minutes are counted—
> don't let me drop dead—
> come quick with the plaster—
> make haste to my bed.

Oh see how already—
my breath's—failing faster—
Herr Doktor, make haste now—
a plaster, a plaster!

—In Karl Kraus it is two war reporters who watch the dying man stretched on the rack; they could take him to a hospital but don't, for they have something positive to tell him, 'Your heroic death will make a fine news item'; and they have a vision too: 'It'll have quite an impact / to show our readership / the priest in the act / of bending o'er his dying lips!'

Black putrefaction; red clouds.

Fiducit!

Occident, a lovely landscape even after the battle: the golden branches of night and stars, inverse image, up above, of the golden plain, and the flutes of autumn resound: Who is coming?—An apparition seen before in a similar landscape, as the herdsmen buried the sun in the bare woods: *Again in lunar stone the brow turns to night; / The sister appears / A radiant youth in autumn and black putrefaction.*—Then she was the Other to black putrefaction and the blackness was merely a veil before her splendour, but what comes swaying towards Grodek is the sister's shadow, and it too goes mutely, as the shadows go that under the sun are the body's silhouette and under the moon are the souls of the dead.— The shadow realm; a Greek landscape, the realm that Odysseus travelled after Circe released him, the realm of the dead, none of whom are dead in the sense of extinction: they have *merely* lost their body, instrument of their activity, have *merely* been thrown into inefficacy, bodiless, deedless shadows, 'fluttering visions', unable ever to leave another mark, yet hungering and howling for activity, for that Other world to the unliveable lives of which Trakl's verses speak—does the reader hear Homer's words, dead Achilles contesting the comforting assertion that he, once the most glorious hero up above, rules mighty as a king down here in the shadow realm?

> Nay, seek not to speak soothingly to me of death, glorious Odysseus. I should choose, so I might live on earth, to serve as the hireling of another, of some portionless man whose livelihood was but small, rather than to be lord over all the dead that have perished . . . [84]

This shadowy realm of the howling souls is the night when no man can work, and the black putrefaction in which all roads end always struck us less as material destruction than as the obliteration of creativity, of the opportunity for human development, of choice and alternatives.—Stagnation; existence stalled; a putrefaction that brings forth nothing, reproducing only itself without cease.—The Trakl poem knows a green putrefaction as well; it exists only in nature but is embedded in life, and from it life shall grow once more: *Soul sang death, the green corruption of the flesh / And it was the murmur / of the woods, / The fervent lamentations of the deer.*—This comes in Trakl's requiem 'To One Who Died Prematurely'; ah, again and yet again: too soon! Now he sees this Too Soon loom before mankind; in the black putrefaction green hope perishes and even the sister is nothing but a shadow now: *To greet the heroes' spirits, their bleeding heads; / And the dark flutes of autumn resound softly in the reeds.*—Dead Pan's farewell.

We confess that the conclusion of this poem, regarded as difficult and enigmatic, never caused us real difficulties; we had it from the start, though never claiming to have it entirely. *O prouder grief! you iron altars / Today the spirit's hot flame is fed by a vast pain, / The grand-children unborn.* 'Prouder'—to which grief is this grief compared? To the lament of the broken mouths? Or to that empty phrase from the newspaper death notices, when a husband's or a brother's or a son's heroic death is mourned? We do not know, we only know that it is prouder than another grief;[85] not 'the proudest', that would be hubris, but prouder, for example, than any comfort.

We have always felt an incredible power emanating from these two words, closely akin to the magnificence of scorn, bracing someone to look his reality in the face, be it a Medusa's head.—This prouder grief is no lament for the past; for the shadows that would be senseless, though now they can know the whole truth about the past; and it is not the grief over a wretched Today in which the shadows yearn to work—it is the grief over the future prepared for the grandchildren, namely, to go unborn. —The word *grandchildren* is surely not restricted to the generation after the next, the children's children; it includes posterity as a whole, a collective term for all genders and all ages; the words 'children', 'sons', 'daughters' would be too specific. *Grandchildren* has a touch of Trakl's favoured neuter, it is all those who can or could come after us, and the word *unborn* has a twofold meaning: 'not yet born' or 'with no possibility of being born'—those who should have sired them are putrefying down in the willow vale. And in Trakl that word *unborn* has yet a third meaning: those who were born into life but could not become the people they were determined to be: *Silver sank the head of one unborn*—this unborn one was named Kaspar Hauser, he was thirty years old and his aspiration was: *to become a cavalryman.* —He did not become one; the murderers came; 'too soon' says the same thing as 'unborn'; unable to become what one could be, unable to unfold one's ability.

These victims, unborn, living, dead—the prouder grief is for them, prouder than the grief of the newspaper notices. We must confess that we cannot stand before the monument of these last three lines without profound emotion: in the vastness of the East the array of altars of iron, not stone, and upon the iron, fed by pain as oil feeds the pylon's flame, the fire of the spirit: does it move matter too? Then the altar glows, an elevated grate, opposite it the other glow, fed by human flesh: beyond

Grodek is Troy, beyond Grodek is Auschwitz; and in the light of these three fires of the Occident, each must face Trakl's poem alone.

As I studied the world Trakl lived in, memories of my childhood trip revived; they passed like shadows through my mind, sometimes crystallizing into a detail; a stone faun's head against taxus hedges; a fountain from which a bellowing horse reared; a snow-white wooden pub table—was it memory, or Trakl's poem? But behind all the rising and drifting images, there was one that emerged again and again, shadowed, blurred, obscurely oppressive: the prisoner in the stone cell, the bars, the pitcher of water, the straw on the floor, the form of the prisoner himself; I saw these things as in tormenting dreams, the more elusive the more urgent your gaze— who was this prisoner? I had seen him, I could swear to it; I'd seen him in the rock, I'd stood before his dungeon, I'd rattled his bars, I shuddered to think of it: was he *the madman*; was I?

My desire to revisit these magical places grew over-powering, but at the same time other jolts came, greater, closer, of the kind that tremble in Trakl's last poems. Once I had made my selection, I read nothing more by Trakl—for five years, I believe—but all the more by Marx and Hegel, and to live up to the demands of the day, I practiced the art of the essay. Then Reclam Verlag, in Leipzig, asked me once again to edit Trakl's work and this time I not only accepted but I also offered to write down my experience and set forth one condition: a trip to Trakl's city.

In May 1977, I travelled to Salzburg; taking the quickest route given by the timetable, I would arrive late at night, intending not to look around on my arrival but to head straight for the hotel and go to sleep and in the morning let the sight of the city flood me like a philtre of memory.

I arrived at midnight; the station was in the New Town, the hotel in the Old Town on the far side of the river, I had seen that much from the map, but as the taxi drove me through the city there was no need to close my eyes; darkness shrouded it, lights sparse, the streets dark, the churches dark, the squares dark, the bridge dark, the sky gloomy and starless; and then my room was a cell— four strides each way, bed, chair, wardrobe, night table —in keeping with my hard currency budget; and when I woke up early in the morning, my first sight of Salzburg was a light shaft, for the room was in the back, the side wall of the shaft intersected the window frame and the opposite wall was not an arm's length away. I could have touched it, a grey, grainy wall, with a chink of grey sky above and grey stone at the bottom.—Bells.—I asked the concierge about Trakl's birthplace; he'd never heard the name before.—Good coffee, ravishing rolls; then the street outside the hotel, it, too, a light shaft, so narrow that a fiacre filled it, and on both sides seven-storey buildings; bells; the shops still closed, delivery trucks, handcarts, dishwater, suddenly a square; suddenly a crush of people; suddenly I stood by the river's channel, the grey Salzach raged down its stony bed, a dull trickle coming from the mouths of the wastewater pipes, but in the air was a scent of snow, the wild Salzach smelt of glaciers, and then a gust of wind rent the clouds, whirled them off down the river, and the mountains emerged, towering over the city, and you fall to your knees.

Not since the Caucasus, thirty years before, had I seen mountains, mountains of rock, unforested, snowy peaks; they seemed to grow up from the zinc of the roofs and the crystalline sky stretched over them; the castle's stone beneath the mountains' stone and at its feet the stone of the city.—The din of thousands of bells; the day got underway.—I forgot my childhood excursion, all I saw was Trakl's poems, I saw their blue, I saw their sky, I saw their city, saw Trakl's colours: blue, brown, violet, red, green, white, hyacinth, gold, rose, opalescence, the colours of Salzburg, the colours of its stone, baroque colours. I saw the verses of this city that were verses from Trakl's poetry: steeds rising from the fountain, the sun's charioteer plunging from the sky, the shadow of the steeple and a gleam of gold at flower-framed windows, the Mönchsberg and the Mirabell Garden, a satyr's dead eyes strayed, escutcheons of royalty, and again and again, and all of this—the stone that was the landscape, enclosing the landscape.

Then the house where Trakl was born; the house where Trakl lived: the courtyard arcades and the pillars in the entry hall; his sister's garden, still growing wild, a walnut tree, elder bushes, weathering fountains; Trakl's pharmacy; Trakl's drugs; Trakl's sun; I walked as in a dream. Café Glockenspiel; Café Tomaselli; the brothel just around the corner on Judengasse had been destroyed in an air raid, but you could look over to the new one, in the rock of the Kapuzinerberg.—*Claws of blossom in the branches*: in the Trakl Archive I saw yellowed photographs and indeed, there stood chestnut trees; and the hospital; and Anif; the suburb; the barred windows and the madness behind them; a dark street, a brown garden, and all at once the canal spat fleshy blood.

I know, now it's time to recall the words of Goethe, that whoever would understand the poet must travel to the poet's land, but today, all too often, these words are arrogance and mockery.—I am not entitled to travel on behalf of readers who are not free to follow my route; I cannot lend them my eyes; Trakl's poem seeks to enter Trakl's landscape, not someone else's much poorer words.—I have no desire to follow the well-known example of that traveller to Sweden who claimed to be traveling for all of us to let us know it isn't worth it.— And so I will tell no more of Salzburg (and nothing of Innsbruck and nothing of Vienna); only this much: that the nuns still hurry, and the föhn wakes a madness you never knew dwelt beneath your brow, and the colour of this madness is black and it drifts down the river to the north, where the slaughterhouses are.

And this too: when I left Trakl's pharmacy (I'd wanted to inquire about the former *Rezeptuarius*, but couldn't utter a word), I climbed the stairs of the lane, narrow as a man, that lead up the Kapuzinerberg and then, halfway up, there it was: the cave in the rock, the bars before it and deep in the rock the prisoner in his hair shirt, bound in chains, a pitcher of water, straw, and nettles, and a frame of ivy, and stone thorns, and living thorns, nature and man's work in the balance, and the bars red with rust. It was the Stations of the Cross that edged this arduous ascent, the *dark Calvary* scaled by *Sebastian Dreaming*: . . . *held by his father's hard hand, and in dim niches in the rock / The man's blue form walked through his legend, / The blood ran purple from the wound beneath the heart. / O how quietly the cross rose in the dark soul.*—It was not rediscovery alone that moved me with the force of the föhn, it was the realization of the singular mystery that lies buried in each person's childhood.—*In his grave the white magician is playing with his serpents.*—A mystery remains a mystery, even your own, to you, and in its darkly growing glow to become Other means: to reconcile the irreconcilable in an indivisible person.—Suddenly I grasped, in Trakl's poems of childhood, that manic and manically constant invocation of his so very near past, the desperate search for the I, for the moment when it became that Other who stares at him and us from the oval frame as the man who has murdered himself.—*Pureness*! *Pureness*! *Where are the dreadful paths of death*, / *Of grey stone silence, the cliffs of the night*, / *And where are the unquiet shades*? *Shining sun-gulf.* // *Sister, when I found you by a lonely glade* / *In the woods, at noon, and the animal's silence was vast*; / *White form beneath the wild oak, and the thorn bloomed silver.* / *Prodigious dying and the singing flame in the heart.*—In the face of childhood, guilt becomes innocence and guilt rebounds upon innocence; I can recall no other poetic *oeuvre* that found such an image for this contradiction: *Shining sun-gulf*.

—Here I understood it, and all at once I grasped this line as well: *Mountains*: *blackness, silence and snow*.

Until then I had seen a person's evolution as a sequence, albeit in a process of unfolding; now, before this cave in the rock and in my memory, before this prisoner in the cold and the chains, I realized that this evolution is also a simultaneity: you lose nothing of what you once were, and you always have been what you are yet to become.—My childhood was fifty years remote, so unfathomably Other, yet suddenly it was closer than my Today from which I stepped into the past: my Catholic childhood, my pious childhood, my childhood with a guardian angel and the Virgin, my Austrian childhood, my Bohemian childhood, my German childhood, my Occidental childhood, my childhood in the mountains, my childhood in the forests, my childhood in the garden, my childhood in the snow, my childhood in the crystal of the heavens, my childhood by a live inferno, my childhood in innocence at my sister's side; my childhood in the Hell ruled by Father and Mother, relentlessly tearing each other apart, relentlessly wringing pain from each other, relentlessly holding us children as shields; my childhood in the village, my childhood in the pub, my childhood in the monastery, my childhood among the Jesuits, my childhood among the Fascists, my childhood with Sindbad, my childhood before the pentagram, my childhood before the crematorium ovens—and I heard the question of a great teacher, St Augustine: Your childhood has gone, but where did it go?—It passed into your mystery; there it is preserved, and the more you remember of it, the darker it becomes to you.—My childhood, too, before this cave; I was ten years old when I stood here, and I recalled that much later I'd written a poem beginning with a dungeon in the rock, after Khrushchev's speech on Stalin; I heard laughter, the slap of waves; was I in the Alps or in the Caucasus?

But I digress: I climbed Calvary; a stone bench, the city far below. I opened the book I always carried with me here, but the lines blurred; I felt that someone was watching me, I glanced up and there sat the angel on the crumbling wall that circles the Kapuzinerberg. Hands around his drawn-up knees, he rocked above the sun-gulf; white sweat dripped from his lids and he wiped it away with one wing.—He smiled; he was home, *he* had found his home, back from the cold north, and I knew that I would lose him now.—What could we have to say to each other?—The lovely city lay below, the splendour of its palaces, the splendour of its history, the splendour of its churches, the splendour of its dynasties—the city that travellers call one of Europe's three most beautiful. Between castle and river the stone of the Old Town; the New Town spreading stony across the plain along the river, a city that turns the lights out early each night, after the arduous daily routine of hard work, what do you know of Austria! You too, angel of my Fatherland; ah, no longer my Fatherland, that lay beneath the ruins of childhood, rats on sooty bricks, and the föhn blustered black through the city.—I had never known the föhn before: all the colours turned febrile, the inconceivable green of a slope that lanced up brighter and brighter, toxic May-green over the green of the cupolas, corrupt copper bloom, from the grey stone burst the thousand colours that slumber in granite and marble, the snow blinding beneath the glowing sky, scorching blue; never before had I seen this.—The river seethed, its vapours fogged my veins; purple veils before my eyes, already obscuring the angel.—A hammering in the skull, a piercing din; the gulf below fumed as sound and fury.— I staggered down the mountain's steps and monks ascended towards me, black, brown, white habits, Franciscans, Augustinians, Capuchins, Jesuits, seeming to spiral their way from the crag; in the rock were the churches; in the rock was the brothel.—An enormous cat in a chalk-white window; the incomprehensible rippling of cars, or were those flags, the city flying flags of black, the raging of the bells, and that night I had a dream: horses rose from a fountain and tumbled me through the city's stone and plunged me into the red-frothing Salzach which closed its stony bed over me.

At breakfast I read about the föhn in the newspaper; it seemed to have been severe, with deaths in traffic, and I imagined a missing-person report: one angel, elderly, faeces-stained wings, inflamed eyelids; I would never see him again.—I went to Hellbrunn, to the trick fountains, that excursion with Father and Mother: stone chairs that squirted water when you sat, goldfish ponds, peacocks and swans; a house as a town full of hardworking people, hammering, sawing, cooking, coopering, neat and industrious and unflagging; I recalled nearly every marionette, but I'd forgotten the rivers that flow into the underworld: blue water into black night.—And then Apollo and Marsyas, hand-sized in one of the dioramas that line the path to the Orpheus Grotto: at the pressing of a button the god lifts his knife and, in horrible jerks, cuts the skin from poor Silenus' body.—I had already written my tale about it; I shuddered; I asked for a photograph.—Soon I got a room in the front of the hotel; behind the windows across the way was a black old-fashioned office.—Gulls screeched in Anif.—Gigantic clocks.—Those who knew Trakl are no longer living.

Have we come closer to understanding Trakl's poetry?

We hope so, yet we fear that to the degree we have approached it, it has eluded us again. The first encounter is usually the most intense, but it is unrepeatable: it makes us desire to understand the poem, to have it wholly as our own, but the more we understand of a poetic *oeuvre*, the more resplendent, a dark fire, does its unilluminable mystery emerge.

Walther Killy, to whom we owe several exemplary essays on Trakl, lucidly formulated the contradiction inherent in understanding such poetry: 'This poetry does not actually seek to be understood content-wise. But one cannot apprehend its musicality and structure except through its content.'[86] And: 'The French, with Baudelaire, Rimbaud and Mallarmé, have long since learnt to attempt different modes of understanding than the "classic" ones; and if German poetry had more figures of Trakl's standing, we too would be forced to do so to a greater degree.'[87]

We have tried to communicate to the reader our experience with Trakl's poem; this communication was itself a new experience, as some things grew clear to us for the first time as we wrote, while other things that seemed clear grew dimmer and dimmer, and new questions have emerged, some as mere intuition, some already as fear.—What dominates is the sense of inadequacy: we have so much more to communicate, so much we feel is essential; what we have achieved seems nothing more than groundwork.—Nothing on 'Helian', nothing on 'Sebastian', nothing on 'The Boy Elis', who emerges from a copper mine of E. T. A. Hoffmann; so little about poetry and dreams, about the truth of both, about the lie of both—no, not 'lie', the precise word is lacking. Perhaps: the contradiction of wish fulfilment, which a poem, like a dream, both is and is not. We had hoped to explore this; we had planned to mirror the *dance of death by pale children* in the poetry of Trakl's contemporaries; we intended to say more about Otto Weininger, including his philosophy of colour; and Rimbaud's philosophy of colour; and Goethe's philosophy of colour, and other links between Goethe and Trakl; we wanted to discuss the influence of Hölderlin; we wanted to speak of the riddle posed to posterity by Trakl's self-portrait, a canvas painted by his own hand, counterpart to the picture in the oval frame, self-portrait of one unborn, self-portrait of one in Hell, self-portrait of one who destroys himself, Kaspar Hauser merged with his murderer, but our strength is exhausted and so, no doubt, is the reader's.

We have lost a faithful companion; we don't know if the angel will find his way back; we don't know who will take his place.—Perhaps Elis.—Trakl's poem will never leave us now; we will continue pondering the truth.

More pain?

We will find out.

But there seems no other way it can be.

Translator's Note

Unless otherwise noted, all translations of the works cited are my own.

I would take this opportunity to thank Uljana Wolf for her feedback on the translation.

Notes

1 *Wörter* refers to 'words' in the technical, quantitative sense, as a collection of grammatical units without regard to deeper meaning or connotation. Thus, a dictionary is a *Wörterbuch* and a computer will calculate the word count or number of *Wörter* in a document. *Worte* emphasizes words, in a complex sense, as units of meaning and vehicles of thought: *Goethes Worte*. *Wort* in this connection can be a pars pro toto, referring to a multiword unit of meaning, a phrase or sentence—as Fühmann calls it here, a 'coined thought'. *Ein Wort Goethes* is likely to refer to an entire Goethe quote. Certain English usages (God's Word, good word, word of honour, have a word with) reflect a similarly broad understanding of the 'word'. [Trans.]

2 Refers to Rainer Maria Rilke poem 'Aus einer Sturmblatt', from *Das Buch der Bilder*. Available in German at: https://goo.gl/pklSuF (last accessed on 22 April 2017). [Trans.]

3 Friedrich Nietzsche, 'The Night Song', in *Thus Spake Zarathustra* (Thomas Common trans.) (New York: Modern Library, 1917), p. 113. [Trans.]

4 Nietzsche, 'The Second Dance Song', in *Thus Spake Zarathustra*, pp. 255–6. [Trans.]

5 Johann Wolfgang von Goethe, *Faust* (Walter Kaufmann trans.) (New York: Anchor Books, 1990), pp. 469–70. [Trans.]

6 Karl Röck, *Tagebuch 1891–1946*, [Diary, 1891–1946] VOL. 1 (Christine Kofler ed.) (Salzburg: Otto Müller Verlag, 1976), p. 240. Available in German at: https://goo.gl/cq8Wx1 (last accessed on 19 April 2017). [Trans.]

7 See Aleksandr Blok's poem entitled 'Twelve', translated from the Russian by Maria Carlson. Available at: https://goo.gl/paZp7U (last accessed on 19 April 2017); here, p. 14. [Trans.]

8 Martin Luther, *Luther's Commentary on the First Twenty-Two Psalms* (Henry Cole trans., John Nicholas Lenker ed.) (Minneapolis: Lutherans in All Lands Co., 1903), pp. 11–13. Available at: https://goo.gl/JgYzRF (last accessed on 19 April 2017). [Trans.]

9 Johann Gottfried Herder, *The Spirit of Hebrew Poetry* (James Marsh trans.) (Burlington: Edward Smith, 1833), p. 41. Available at: https://goo.gl/QquVlS (last accessed on 19 April 2017). [Trans.]

10 P. Mansell Jones, 'Baudelaire as a Critic of Contemporary Poetry', in *Modern Miscellany Presented to Eugène Vinaver by Pupils, Colleagues and Friends* (T. E. Lawrenson, F. E. Sutcliffe and G. F. A. Gadoffre eds) (New York: Manchester University Press, 1969), p. 147–8. [Trans.]

11 Hugo Friedrich, *The Structure of Modern Poetry* (Joachim Neugroschel trans.) (Evanston: Northwestern University Press, 1974), p. 140. [Trans.]

12 Ibid., p. 125. [Trans.]

13 Ibid. [Trans.]

14 Friedrich Hölderlin, 'Stuttgart', in *Odes and Elegies* (Nick Hoff trans. and ed.) (Middletown: Wesleyan University Press, 2008), p. 120–7. [Trans.]

15 Ibid., p. 214. [Trans.]

16 Hölderlin, 'Dying for the Fatherland', in *Odes and Elegies*, p. 55. [Trans.]

17 *Mond* means 'moon', *Mohn* means 'poppy', *Mund* means 'mouth' and *Mord* means 'murder'. [Trans.]

18 Charles Baudelaire, 'Spleen', in *The Poems and Prose Poems of Charles Baudelaire* (F. P. Sturm trans.) (New York: Brentano's, 1919), p. 36. Available at: https://goo.gl/c2sJXf (last accessed on 19 April 2017). [Trans.]

19 Cf. *Georg Trakl, Gedichte: Ausgewählt und interpretiert von Albrecht Weber* [Georg Trakl, Poems: Selected and Interpreted by Albrecht Weber] (Munich: Kösel-Verlag, 1957).

20 In Rilke's famous poem 'Closing Piece', it is this very position that is abandoned—or, rather, it is the abandonment of this position that is expressed: 'Death is great. / We are his completely / with laughing eyes. / When we feel ourselves immersed in life, / he dares to weep / immersed in us.'—Rainer Maria Rilke, *The*

Book of Images (Edward Snow trans.) (Berkeley: North Point Press, 1994), p. 253.

This highly precise '*feel ourselves* immersed in life' reflects that very false consciousness, the inability to endure 'what is'.

21 Rainer Maria Rilke's poem, 'Der Tod', in *Insel-Almanach auf das Jahr 1919* (Munich: Insel Verlag, 1919). Available in German at: https://goo.gl/m3S9rN (last accessed on 19 April 2017). [Trans.]

22 See Edvard Munch, 'MM UT 13: "The Origins of the Frieze of Life." Oslo, 1928' (Francesca M. Nichols trans.), in *Edvard Munch's Writings* (Digital Archive: Munch Museum, 2012). Available at: https://goo.gl-/N01p8I (last accessed on 19 April 2017). [Trans.]

23 Gottfried Benn, 'Can Poets Change the World', in *Gottfried Benn: Prose, Essays, Poems* (Joel Agee trans.) (New York: Continuum, 1987), p. 101–102. [Trans.]

24 T. S. Eliot, 'Tradition and the Individual Talent', in *The Sacred Wood and Major Early Essays* (Mineola: Dover Publications, 1998), p. 33. [Trans.]

25 Goethe, *Faust*, p. 161. [Trans.]

26 Friedrich Nietzsche, *The Will to Power* (Walter Kaufmann and R. J. Hollingdale trans) (New York: Vintage, 1968), p. 112. [Trans.]

27 Ibid., p. 105. [Trans.]

28 Le Comte de Lautréamont, *Maldoror and Poems* (Paul Knight trans.) (London: Penguin Books, 1988), p. 153. [Trans.]

29 Nikita Khrushchev's speech, 'On the Cult of Personality and Its Consequences', at the 20th Congress of the C. P. S. U. in February 1956, denounced the crimes and 'personality cult' of the Stalin era and set the process of de-Stalinization in motion. [Trans.]

30 Trakl's poems 'Psalm' and 'De profundis' feature the repetition of the phrase *Es ist*, whose ambiguity is difficult to render in English. Literally it means 'it is' but its meaning can shift to a more general 'there is'. The Biblical 'let there be light' is '*es werde Licht*'. As Fühmann alludes to Genesis, and later to Rimbaud's phrase, '*il y a*' which most English translators have rendered as 'there is', I have translated *Es ist* throughout as 'there is'. [Trans.]

31 I am indebted here to Reinhold Grimm's instructive articles: 'Ein Wegbereiter' [A Forerunner], in *Strukturen* (Göttingen: Sachse und Pohl, 1963); and 'Georg Trakls Verhältnis zu Rimbaud', in *Germanisch-Romanische Monatsschrift*, New Series, VOL. 9 (Heidelberg: University of Heidelberg, 1959).

32 Vítězslav Nezval, 'Woman in Plural', in Jerome Rothenberg, *Writing Through: Translations and Variations* (Middletown: Wesleyan University Press, 2004), p. 40. [Trans.]

33 Arthur Rimbaud, 'Childhood', in *Poems* (Paul Schmidt trans.) (New York: Alfred A. Knopf, 1994), p. 129–34. [Trans.]

34 Vítězslav Nezval, 'Prague in the Midday Sun' (Ewald Osers trans.), in *Against Forgetting: Twentieth-Century Poetry of Witness* (Carolyn Forché ed.) (New York: W. W. Norton, 1993), p. 416–18. The lines beginning with 'Like . . . ' here, begin with '*Es ist*' in Fühmann's translation. [Trans.]

35 Joseph von Eichendorff, 'Der Jäger Abschied'. Available in German at: https://goo.gl/ly9MBr (last accessed on 19 April 2017). [Trans.]

36 Homer, 'Hymn 18. To Pan', in *The Homeric Hymns: A New Prose Translation; and Essays, Literary and Mythological* (Andrew Lang ed. and trans.) (George Allen, 1899). Available at: https://goo.gl/kBYLY2 (last accessed on 19 April 2017). [Trans.]

37 Heinrich Heine, *Ludwig Börne: A Memorial* (Jeffrey L. Sammons trans.) (Rochester: Camden House, 2006), p. 27. [Trans.]

38 Ibid., p. 43. [Trans.]

39 Ibid., p. 36. [Trans.]

40 Arthur Rimbaud, *Rimbaud Complete* (Wyatt Mason ed. and trans.) (New York: Modern Library Classics, 2003), pp. 12–16. [Trans.]

41 Heine and Rimbaud felt this disenchantment with particular bitterness as regards sexuality, seeking in

Christianity the reasons for eroticism's impoverishment, but we will not examine this further, if only because here Trakl's stance is utterly (and uniquely) different; recall how he quotes Christ: 'The twain shall be one flesh', and his 'Rosary Songs'.

42 Karl Marx, *Grundrisse: Foundations of the Critique of Political Economy* (Martin Nicolaus trans.) (London: Penguin Books, 1993), p. 111. [Trans.]

43 Rimbaud, *Rimbaud Complete*, p. 229. [Trans.]

44 Walter Killy, *Über Georg Trakl* (Göttingen: Vandenhoeck and Ruprecht, 1960).

45 From Georg Trakl, *Sebastian im Traum* [Sebastian Dreaming] (Leipzig: Kurt Wolff Verlag, 1915). For English translation of this collection of poems see Georg Trakl, *Sebastian Dreaming* (James Reidel trans.) (London: Seagull Books, 2016). [Trans.]

46 Reinhold Grimm points to an equivalent in Rimbaud's 'First Communion': 'Every century they dress up these barns / With a coat of blueing and curdled milk: / If mystic freakshows are worth a look-see [. . .]'. He deserves thanks for pointing it out; however, Trakl has 'milk', not 'curdled milk' (Rimbaud: 'lait caillé'), a fine example of appropriation as transformation. [English translation: Arthur Rimbaud, 'First Communion', in *Rimbaud: The Works* (Dennis J. Carlile trans.) (Xlibris Corporation, 2000), p. 126.]

47 At the 1976 Salzburg Trakl Symposium, Professor Bernhard Böschenstein from Geneva expressed the

hope that *the madman* in Trakl's 'Psalm' might refer to Hölderlin, citing a variant of the first version: *Behind him stands his brother, a sad fellow who died in green Swabia.*—But *Swabia* is not only Hölderlin's birthplace; Trakl's paternal ancestors came from a different Swabia, the region of Hungary settled by Germans. Trakl had unknown relatives there, and these Swabians were on his mind, as shown by a variant of his poem 'The Ramble' in which the beginning of the fifth stanza:

> *Your brother dies in a cursed land*

goes:

> *Your brother dies far away in Hungary-land*
> > *Swabia-land;*
> > *Hungary-land*

That's the rub of poetry: it is never fully covered by one interpretation.

48 Otto Basil, *Georg Trakl in Selbstzeugnissen und Bilddokumenten* [Georg Trakl in Personal Testimonials and Photographic Documents] (Reinbek: Rowohlt, 1965).

49 Stephan Hermlin [1915–97] was active in the Communist resistance in the 1930s, then went into exile in France, Switzerland and Palestine. After the war he returned to Germany to become one of the GDR's most prominent writers, though he became increasingly critical of the regime in later years. [Trans.]

50 Grete Trakl [1891–1917], a gifted pianist, began studying under Ernst von Dohnányi in Berlin in 1910;

nothing is known of her husband, Arthur Langen, except for the date of their wedding: 17 July 1912.

51 From 'Anaximander', in *Early Greek Philosophy* (Jonathan Barnes trans. and ed.) (London: Penguin Books, 2001), p. 21. [Trans.]

52 Karl Röck, *Tagebuch 1891–1946*. The abbreviations: MAX = Café Maximilian in Innsbruck, E = the cartoonist Max von Esterle, Fi = Ludwig von Ficker, Kr = Karl Kraus. Georg Trakl is denoted by 'T'; in the following quotes I always write out his name.—In 1919, Karl Röck published Georg Trakl's collected poems in an outlandish arrangement of cycles whose bureaucratic rationale confirms that for all his closeness to Trakl he remained a stranger to him: he attempted in all seriousness to tease apart the unities of contradiction according to unambiguous concepts and match them with prosodic elements, in short, to establish a 'Trakl formula'; for a long time his efforts were seen as exemplary.

53 Speaking of 'Borneo' and 'Java', readers may welcome a stanza by the Czech poet Vitězslav Nezval, from his 'Poetika': 'We're rabble from the gutters / A bunch of athletes whores poets / And off to Siam you can't / Stand it at home any more'. One could also mention Konstantin Biebl, who found his Bohemia only on Java; and of course, above all, Gauguin.

54 Ludwig Wittgenstein, two years younger than Trakl, said of his poetry: 'I don't understand it, but its tone delights me. It is the tone of a true genius.'

55 **Dr** Franz Schwab [1886–1956], a doctor and school-friend of Trakl's.

56 **Paula** von Ficker, Rudolf von Ficker's wife; in a letter **to** her husband from 15 November 1913.

57 [In 1912, Karl Kraus' letter was published in *Die Fackel*.]

> Only seven-month-old children blame their parents with their gaze, making them huddle, like thieves caught red-handed, alongside their victims. They have the gaze that demands what was taken from them, and when their thoughts drift off, it is as though to seek the rest, as they stare backward into omission. There are others who consciously assume such a gaze, but a gaze that wishes to pay back to chaos the excess they have received. These are the perfect ones, completed when it was too late. With a cry of shame they emerged into a world which has left them only the one, first, ultimate feeling: Back into your womb, o mother, where all was good! With thanks to Georg Trakl for the Psalm—Karl Kraus.

58 Carl Dallago [1869–1949], philosopher and member of the *Der Brenner* staff.

59 Hans Limbach, 'Begegnung mit Trakl', in *Erinnerung an Georg Trakl: Zeugnisse und Briefe*, 3rd EDN (Ludwig von. Ficker ed.) (Salzburg: Otto Müller Verlag, 1966). Reprinted by the permission of the Brenner-Archiv, Innsbruck. [Trans.]

60 This example shows how legends come into being: in his *Erinnerungen eines Bibliothekars* (Weimar, 1925), Richard Kukula claims that a medical orderly 'saw though the keyhole how the Lieutenant' (Trakl) 'lying in his sickbed tore the bandages from his wounds and pounded his body with his fists . . .'—Trakl was never wounded.

61 The term 'Fiducit' is derived from a Latin expression, here it refers to a German fraternity ritual: when two men drink to pledge brotherhood, one says 'Schmollis' (from 'sis mihi mollis amicus', be my close friend), and the other replies 'Fiducit' (from 'fiducia sit', let it be so). [Trans.]

62 Ludwig von Ficker, 'Der Abschied', in *Erinnerung an Georg Trakl*. Reprinted by the permission of the Brenner-Archiv, Innsbruck.

63 Roth may be referring to the Polish hospital staff, whom he accused of mishandling Trakl's case. Ethnic tensions within Austro-Hungary were high before and during the First World War. [Trans.]

64 Ludwig von Ficker pointed out that Mathias Roth must have mistaken the date: Trakl died in the night of 4/5 November 1914.

65 Ludwig von Ficker, 'Der Abschied', in *Erinnerung an Georg Trakl*. Reprinted by the permission of the Brenner-Archiv, Innsbruck.

66 Stephan Hermlin, Afterword in *Georg Trakl: Gedichte* (Leipzig: Reclam, 1975).

67 Friedrich Nietzsche, *Human, All Too Human* (Gary Handwerk trans.) (Stanford: Stanford University Press, 2000), p. 68. [Trans.]

68 From Georg Trakl, *Georg Trakl, Dichtungen und Briefe*, VOL. 2 (Walter Killy and Hans Szklenar eds) (Salzburg: Otto Müller Verlag, 1969), pp. 68–9.

69 Ludwig von Ficker, *Denkzettel und Danksagungen. Aufsätze, Reden* (Munich: Kösel, 1967).

70 Jacob and Wilhelm Grimm, 'Little Brother and Little Sister', in *Household Tales* (Margaret Hunt trans.) (London: George Bell, 1884, 1892), p. 352. [Trans.]

71 Plato, *The Laws of Plato* (Thomas L. Pangle trans.) (Chicago: University of Chicago Press, 1988), p. 230. [Trans.]

72 Jacob and Wilhelm Grimm, *Household Tales*, VOL. 1 (Margaret Hunt trans.) (London: George Bell, 1884, 1892), p. 352. [Trans.]

73 Interestingly, some versions of the 'Little Brother and Little Sister' tale link the latent incest with cannibalism: for example, the Hungarian tale magnificently retold by Mrs Palkó-Jozsef, in *Ungarische Volks-märchen* (Gyula Ortutay ed.) (Berlin: Rütten & Loening, 1957).

74 Charles Baudelaire, 'L'Héautontimorouménos' (Roy Campbell trans.), in *Flowers of Evil: A Selection* (Marthiel and Jackson Mathews eds) (New York: New Directions, 1955), p. 69. [Trans.]

75 Otto Weininger, *Sex and Character* (Ladislaus Löb trans., Daniel Steuer and Laura Marcus eds) (Bloomington: Indiana University Press, 2005), p. 97. [Trans.]

76 It may help to recall that 'or' has three meanings. First, 'S or P' can mean 'S and P, or S, or P, but one of the two must be present' (alternative); second, 'Either S, or P, never both together but at least one' (anti-valence); third, 'At most S, or at most P, or neither of the two' (exclusion).—The first is an 'or' of open arms; the second an 'or' in the sense of Cinderella sorting lentils, easily shading into the third 'or', one of twilight and decay.—In 'or' as a *Wort* with the plural *Worte*, all these meanings resonate together: poetic logic says 'true' even where logistical logic must say 'false'.

77 Rainer Maria Rilke, *New Poems* (Leon Krisak trans.) (Rochester: Boydell and Brewer, 2015), p. 225. [Trans.]

78 Rainer Maria Rilke, 'Lament', in *Uncollected Poems* (Edward Snow trans.) (Berkeley: North Point Press, 2014), p. 95. [Trans.]

79 Ibid., p. 173. [Trans.]

80 Refers to the Soviet invasion of Czechoslovakia in August 1968, which crushed the 'Prague Spring' and destroyed hopes of reform throughout the East Bloc. [Trans.]

81 From Johann Wolfgang von Goethe, 'Primal Words, Orphic', in *Selected Poems* (John Whaley trans.)

(Evanston: Northwestern University Press, 1998), pp. 123–5. [Trans.]

82 Literal translation: 'Thorn'; 'grain'; 'bread'; 'red'; 'breath'; 'dwell'; 'death'; 'gold'; 'lap'; 'reeds'; 'murder'; 'moon'; 'poppy'; 'moss'; 'rust'; 'straw'; 'river'; 'frost'; 'wolf'; 'village'; 'food'; 'basket'; 'God'; 'thrush'; 'bell'; 'sun'; 'vaults of thorns'; 'rosy'; 'wave'. [Trans.]

83 Literal translation: 'dripped'; 'melted'; 'bent'; 'lied'; 'died'; 'broke'. [Trans.]

84 Homer, *The Odyssey* (A. T. Murray trans.) (Cambridge: Harvard University Press, 1919). Available at: https://goo.gl/R23UJe (last accessed on 19 April 2017). [Trans.]

85 This is another one of Trakl's idiosyncrasies, akin to his predilection for the neuter form of present participles: the use of the comparative as a starting point, a peculiar heightening effect; it would deserve a thorough evaluation.

86 Walter Killy, *Über Georg Trakl*, p. 34.

87 Ibid., p. 35.